D1524458

The Collected Poems of A.K. Ramanujan

Books in English by A.K. Ramanujan

Poetry

The Striders (1966)
Relations (1971)
Selected Poems (1976)
Second Sight (1986)

Translations

The Interior Landscape: Love Poems from a Classical Tamil Anthology (1967)

Samskara: A Rite for a Dead Man, a translation of U. Anantha Murthy's Kannada novel (1976)

Hymns for the Drowning: Poems for Visnu by Nammalvar, translated from Tamil (1981)

Poems of Love and War: From the Eight Anthologies and the Ten Long Poems of Classical Tamil (1985)

Folktales from India: A Selection of Oral Tales from Twenty-two Languages (1991)

Co-authored and co-edited with others

The Literatures of India: An Introduction (1975), with Edward C. Dimock, Jr., and others

Another Harmony: New Essays on the Folklore of India (1986), with Stuart Blackburn

When God Is a Customer: Telugu Courtesan Songs by Ksetrayya and Others (1994), with V. Narayana Rao and David Shulman

The Oxford Anthology of Modern Indian Poetry (1994), with Vinay Dharwadker

Posthumous

The Black Hen in *The Collected Poems* (1994)
Collected Essays (1995)

The Collected Poems of
A.K. Ramanujan

DELHI
OXFORD UNIVERSITY PRESS
BOMBAY CALCUTTA MADRAS
1995

Oxford University Press, Walton Street, Oxford OX2 6DP

Oxford New York
Athens Auckland Bangkok Bombay
Calcutta Cape Town Dar es Salaam Delhi
Florence Hong Kong Istanbul Karachi
Kuala Lumpur Madras Madrid Melbourne
Mexico City Nairobi Paris Singapore
Taipei Tokyo Toronto
and associates in
Berlin Ibadan

Typeset by Rastrixi, New Delhi 110070
Printed in India at Pauls Press, New Delhi 110020
and published by Neil O'Brien, Oxford University Press
YMCA Library Building, Jai Singh Road, New Delhi 110001

Contents

x

Acknowledgements

Editorial Acknowledgements for *The Black Hen* (1995)

The Black Hen was compiled by

A.L. Becker
Vinay Dharwadker
Edward C. Dimock, Jr.
Keith Harrison
Krittika M. Ramanujan
Molly Daniels-Ramanujan
Alane Rollings
Keith Taylor

Editorial Acknowledgements for *The Collected Poems* (1995)

Vinay Dharwadker, co-editor with A.K. Ramanujan of *The Oxford Anthology of Modern Indian Poetry*, and now General Editor of A.K. Ramanujan's *Collected Essays*; A.L. Becker and Keith Taylor, colleagues, who along with Ramanujan belonged to a poetry writing group in Michigan; Keith Harrison, fellow poet and friend of twenty years from Minnesota; Alane Rollings, poet and friend from Chicago; Edward C. Dimock, Ramanujan's near twin (they were born within a day of each other); and his daughter, Krittika Ramanujan, have all, each and everyone, made it possible to bring out this volume, soon after the first anniversary of the poet's death. Their close connection with him and his work has given assurance to the selection of poems being published posthumously in *The Black Hen*. The first three books of the quartet making up *The Collected Poems* are being reprinted exactly as in the original editions.

Most of all, grateful acknowledgements are due to the Committee on Social Thought and the Department of South Asian

Languages and Civilizations at the University of Chicago, for their continued support; to David Baird for his computer wizardry and generous help; to Ramonda Talkie and Jessie Sheridan for being there at the start.

The editors and publishers of this volume are grateful to the editors of the following magazines for permission to reprint poems that appeared first in their pages, in the last two cases posthumously:

Chicago Review: 'Elegy' and 'Butcher's Tao';

London Poetry Review: 'The Black Hen';

Poetry (Chicago): 'Bosnia' (as 'How Can One Write about Bosnia'), 'Sonnet', 'In March', 'Pain', and 'Foundlings in the Yukon';

World Literature Today: 'Shadows', 'A Report', and 'Some Monarchs and a Wish'.

The publication of *The Collected Poems,* with so many friends actively participating, is a celebration rather than an act of mourning.

Molly Daniels-Ramanujan

Author's Acknowledgements for *The Striders* (1966)

Acknowledgements are due to the editors of the following periodicals and anthologies in which some of these poems have previously appeared: *The Atlantic Monthly, Encounter, Folio, The Illustrated Weekly of India, New England Review, Poetry (Chicago), Poetry Northwest, Quartet, Quest, Thought, The Best Poems of 1961, Young Commonwealth Poets '65,* and *New Voices of the Commonwealth.* The poem 'Anxiety' is © 1961, The Atlantic Monthly Company, Boston, Massachusetts, U.S.A.

'An Image for Politics' was suggested by an image in *Pincher Martin* by William Golding.

The Striders is dedicated to Molly.

Author's Acknowledgements for *Relations* (1971)

Acknowledgements are due to the editors of the following anthologies and periodicals in which some of these poems first appeared: *The Chicago Review, The Illustrated Weekly of India, Indian Writing Today, New York Times, Pergamon Poets, Quest*; also to the following radio and TV stations: WFMT (Chicago), WKPK (Chicago), All India Radio (Delhi, Bangalore), and New Delhi TV.

Among my conscious debts are a phrase from Vinda Karandikar in 'Eyes, Ears, Noses, and a Thing about Touch', one from Pablo Neruda's prose in 'A Lapse of Memory', and an incident from a Kannada magazine story in 'History'.

Relations is dedicated to Molly, Krittika, and Krishna.

Author's Acknowledgements for *Second Sight* (1986)

I am grateful to the editors of the following journals where earlier versions of these poems appeared:

Poetry (Chicago): 'In the Zoo', 'Ecology', 'Death and the Good Citizen';

The Carleton Miscellany: 'Chicago Zen';

The American Scholar: 'Extended Family';

Indian Literature: 'Elements of Composition', 'Looking for the Centre', 'No Amnesia King'.

The phrase 'Not on Thursday, not in Paris' in 'Saturdays' alludes to César Vallejo's poem on his death, 'Black Stone on a White Stone'.

Second Sight is dedicated to David Greene.

Preface

Krittika Ramanujan

A.K. Ramanujan left at his death one hundred and forty-eight poems on three computer disks. Eight editors read the poems, and selected those they thought could go into a volume of collected poems. Poems that were chosen by all or most readers were included in *The Black Hen*, which was then arranged and edited by Molly Daniels. Many of the poems not chosen were clearly publishable, but they seemed more suitable for a volume of uncollected poems.

Ramanujan worked on these poems off and on for years, as was his habit. He often joked that poems were like babies, they dirtied themselves and he had to clean them up. He said it took him ten years to really finish a set of poems.

The earliest of the new poems seem to have been written in 1989, in Michigan, the latest in March or April 1993. Like many poets, A.K. Ramanujan began writing poetry when he was seventeen. At the time he was reading a great deal of English literature from his father's library, English being his third language. His initial interest was in writing plays for the radio. His favourite poets were Shelley and Yeats. While he always loved Yeats, in later life he preferred Wallace Stevens and William Carlos Williams.

The poems in *The Black Hen* are in some ways different from their predecessors. At first reading, they seem light, easy, some almost like exercises. After a few readings, a complete reversal takes place. When the poems are read in sequence, they seem entirely different. The ear begins to hear the voice as full, rhythmic, passionate, complex, changeable, and in a variety of voices, styles and forms. The poems are metaphysical and full of a frightening darkness. There is a sense of both a pressure towards this darkness and a simultaneous revulsion from it. The poems begin to seem denser and fuller than anything the poet had done before, the culmination of forty-seven years of writing poetry. It is almost impossible to avoid the idea that the poems seem to press towards death and disintegration and even beyond to transmutation, like lines drawn from different angles which converge on a single point, without apparent intention, and yet inevitably.

What is astonishing is that the idea of nothingness, of zero, occurs frequently, as in the following lines:

> How describe this nothing
> we, of all things, flee in panic
> yet wish for, work towards,
> build ships and shape whole cities with?

Salamanders

Ramanujan was very interested in Buddhism. (He tried to convert in his twenties.) I think there is here a Buddhist idea of nothingness, as well as perhaps an Existential one.

Animals appear everywhere in the poems, but the poems are not 'about' animals. They have a double *vision*. The poems are about life, death, cycles of birth, pain, and love. They are also about poetry. They are full of irony, humour, paradox and sudden reversals.

A volume of *Collected Poems*, which represents the best work of a lifetime, is a milestone in any poet's path. This volume, which was considered during A.K. Ramanujan's lifetime, is now being published posthumously. *The Collected Poems* consists of three previously published books: *The Striders, Relations,* and *Second Sight,* and a fourth, *The Black Hen* published within a book for the first time. Now, as Auden wrote, may the 'words of a dead man' be 'modified in the guts of the living.'

xvi

Introduction

Vinay Dharwadker

When I first read A.K. Ramanujan's last, unpublished poems several months ago, their impact as individual pieces and as a fortuitous group took me by surprise. In November 1989, in Ann Arbor, Michigan, he had shown me the first few poems he had completed after the publication of *Second Sight* (1986), and in June 1992, in Chicago, he had asked me to read nearly forty poems that he wanted to include in a new collection. But these occasions, among others, did not prepare me for the large number of poems that turned up in his files in the autumn of 1993, or for their unexpected qualities and effects.

As readers of this edition of his *Collected Poems* will discover on their own, Ramanujan's final poems contain elements that are not present in the three volumes of poetry he published in his lifetime. These formal and thematic elements now alter our understanding of what the poet felt and thought, why he chose certain voices, images, and metaphors, what his conceptions of nature and culture were, how he re-imagined time and human history, where he located the conflicts and interdependences of society, family, and self, or how he resolved some of the ethical dilemmas of poetry in the late twentieth century. But even as the finished work enlarges and rearranges his poetic world, it reinforces the continuities between the various phases of his career over three or four decades. It thus creates a new imaginative whole in which late and early poems interact associatively with each other, and long-standing preoccupations combine echoes and resonances with variations and counter-points to achieve an integrity that is at once essential and ironic.

1

One of the recurrent concerns in Ramanujan's poetry as a whole is the nature of the human body and its relation to the natural world. This theme first appears in *The Striders* (1966) in an early sonnet called 'Towards Simplicity', which represents the body as a natural mechanism. The poem suggests that the body is a structure with organic as well as mechanical properties, and consists of parts like 'Corpuscle, skin, / cell, and membrane', each with 'its minute seasons / clocked within the bones'. The body's internal seasons, such as its 'hourly autumn', parallel the external seasonal cycles and establish a relationship of co-ordination between body and nature. But the body's processes are 'minute' and 'complex', while those in nature are 'large' and 'simple'. Besides, the body houses the mind, which possesses unique powers—'reasons gyring within reasons'—that seem to transcend the domain of nature. At the time of death, however, 'into the soil as soil we come', so the body finally subsumes the mind despite the asymmetries between them, and the earth in turn subsumes the body. Since external nature thus controls our internal organic processes and mechanical properties from beginning to end, it completely 'contains' our bodily lives.

'Death and the Good Citizen', written nearly twenty years after 'Towards Simplicity' and included in *Second Sight*, complicates this argument by dramatizing the conflict between three divergent interpretations of the body's place in the natural order. From a modern and secular environmentalist viewpoint, the human body appears to be entirely natural, is contained in nature, and returns after death, or ought to return, to nature. This return is a specific instance of the general principle of conservation, according to which everything in our environment ought to be recycled. During one's lifetime, for example, the body's waste-matter should be collected as 'nightsoil' and used to fertilize, say, orange trees in a municipal garden. Correspondingly, at the time of death the body's healthy organs should be donated for transplants, say, of hearts and eyes. But from an orthodox Hindu viewpoint, an act like organ-donation at death constitutes an unacceptable 'degradation' of the body. The speaker in the poem, caught initially between the conflicting environmentalist and Hindu positions, observes that if he were to die in India and leave his body to a hospital, the members of his 'tribe' of brahmans would 'speak proverbs, contest / my will':

xviii

> they'll cremate
> me in Sanskrit and sandalwood,
> have me sterilized
> to a scatter of ash.

This conflict, however, does not define the limits of his dilemma. He knows that if he were to die in the West, then his desire to recycle his body-parts would also run into difficulties with a third, rather different system of beliefs: from a traditional Christian viewpoint, the body after death should be neither 'dismantled' nor cremated but allowed to 'decompose'. The speaker knows that in keeping with this tradition,

> they'll lay me out in a funeral
> parlour, embalm me in pesticide,
> bury me in a steel trap, lock
> me out of nature
> till I'm oxidized by left-
> over air, withered by my own
> vapours into grin and bone.

So even in the modern West, where secular environmentalism may be widespread but Christian rites of passage still predominate, he will not be free to 'return to nature' as he wishes. He realizes that because of these constraints,

> My tissue will never graft,
> will never know newsprint,
> never grow in a culture,
> or be mould and compost
> for jasmine, eggplant
> and the unearthly perfection
> of municipal oranges.

But he can offer this conclusion only as a mixture of regret and mock-regret, for he knows all too well that he is 'hidebound' and fully 'biodegradable'. No matter whether he is dismantled by secular doctors, cremated by orthodox brahmans, or embalmed and buried by conservative Christians, he will return to nature even in an alien environment, quite thoroughly 'naturalized' in the end.

Other poems in *Second Sight* explore conceptions of the body that break away from the relatively limited concerns of 'Towards Simplicity' and 'Death and the Good Citizen'. 'Love Poem for a Wife and Her Trees', for example, playfully links the human body to three kinds of trees. The first two sections of the poem juxtapose the metaphorical notion that bodily reproduction occurs on the 'branches' of a 'family-tree', with the more mystical notion that the human spinal-cord is itself a tree-like formation inside the body. The third section places these two figurative trees beside an apple tree, making the third tree equally real and mythical, particularly with its ironic resemblance to the tree of knowledge in the garden of Eden. Since the first three parts of the poem are arranged like pieces in a jigsaw game, the relation between body and nature becomes an instance of the trope of metonymy, which equates trees with bodies and bodies with trees.

The mutual penetration of body and natural world that we find in 'Love Poems for a Wife and Her Trees' goes several steps further in 'Looking for the Centre' in the same volume. In the second section of the latter poem, Ramanujan's second-person persona opens 'an old anatomy book'. As he turns over the transparent flaps of superposed diagrams of the body's internal structure, he discovers that the illustration at the very bottom, 'under the crimson // pair of kidneys', is nothing but 'a map / of the heavens'. In the next section of the poem, the self-consciously eccentric speaker undertakes yet one more search for a determinate centre of existential meaning within himself. But this time he undergoes a Kafkaesque metamorphosis and turns into 'a zilla spider // on LSD', who uses his own bodily substance to spin 'enormous webs / in a Tahiti forest of April twigs'. Such surreal moments of revelation and transformation dance between two disparate conceptions of the body-nature relationship: that the solid body of flesh and bone somehow contains the largely empty, mineral heavens, and that the human body, which can never transcend its life in culture, can still be exchanged with the insect or animal body in nature.

The final poems collected here in *The Black Hen* extend the interconnections among body, nature and culture in several unpredictable directions. In 'A Meditation' the speaker enters a trance in which he envisions his aging body as a black walnut tree that topples over in an overnight storm. Next morning, men with saws cut it into pieces and cart it away, and a carpenter uses some of the planks to fashion a table and a chair, while a papermill pulps other parts of the tree to produce writing-paper. The poet, still caught in a meditative trance and very conscious of himself as a ghost walnut tree, slowly grows aware of the multiple bodies and centres of consciousness into which he has been split, processed, and distributed. As various products of the tree and parts of himself return and surround him in the everyday economy of material consumption, he imagines himself sitting

in this chair,
paper and pencil on my table,
and as I write

I know I'm writing now on my head,
now on my torso, my living
hands moving

on a dead one, a firm imagined body
working with the transience
of breathless

real bodies.

Like 'Love Poem to a Wife and Her Trees' and 'Looking for the Centre' in *Second Sight*, 'A Meditation' stretches Ramanujan's sharp-sighted realism towards what can only be called the metaphysical and the mystical, combining the Upanishads and *bhakti* poetry, the Virashaiva tradition in Kannada and the Shrivaishnava tradition in Tamil, Spinoza and Zen Buddhism, and Pascal and Borges. The visionary quality evident in 'In March', another late poem in *The Black Hen*, where the fictional speaker uses an interior monologue to dramatize the delirium caused by high fever and third-degree burns. As he lies in bed, barely aware of his physical self or surroundings, he intensely feels the entire natural world—continents, oceans, dolphins, icebergs, islands, seashores, rivers, alligators, forests, and birds—circulating inside his body. Not only is the body contained in nature, but in an extraordinary, hyperreal state of consciousness all of nature also seems to be contained in the human body.

Perhaps 'One More on a Deathless Theme' contains Ramanujan's final, most fantastic account of the body-nature nexus. The poem is obviously a contemplation of mortality and its bitter and ironic 'deathless theme' is the death of the body. The poet now conceives of the body, regardless of species, as the organic site where birth, copulation, and death come together insuperably. Mixing the literal and the metaphorical and the factual and the mythical, the poem suggests with memorable effect that everybody—every body—is destined to die a dog's death:

> This body I sometimes call me,
> sometimes mine,
> as if I'm someone else
> owning and informing this body . . .
>
> will one day be short of breath,
> lose its thrust,
> turn cold, dehydrate and leave
> a jawbone with half a grin
> near a pond: just as this dog
> I walk
>
> to let him pass water and express his waste
> so he may frisk and slobber happily
> all day, or moan at the gate
> for that female in the street,
> will turn cold
>
> like her and her nuzzling suitors . . .

The poem also implies that the sequence of links from birth and desire to copulation and death, and then beyond death to other births and other deaths, is so long that it spans the entire chain of being in the universe. Besides humans, that chain contains every kind of real and imaginary being. Above the human level, it includes the minor and major gods, from 'our god / who used to be everywhere but now is housed / in the kitchen' to the great, androgynous 'God Whose One Half / is Woman'. Below the human domain, the chain interlinks' mammal and quadruped' and even contains

> the bluebottles on the dog-do
> begetting bluebottles
>
> on bluebottles, those sapphires
> among flies,
> and the praying mantis astride
> on another praying mantis,
> green and still on the seasoned
> apple tree . . .

Trapped in this cosmic hierarchy levelled by death, 'all these people in this street / and all the other streets everywhere' will 'become cold, lie under stones / or be scattered as ash / in rivers and oceans'. Death thus becomes the supreme irony in life, one which finally consumes both the individual human body and the complete order of animate nature. The clock that ticks inside the natural mechanism of any living body is also the clock ticking away in the natural world outside, and it is the nature of this universal clock to tick inexorably towards the terminal irony of death.

2

An exploration of the 'co-extension' of the human body and nature leads to a concern with natural processes in general and the more abstract issues concerning time. The early poems in *The Striders* refer more than once to the notion that the body and its parts maintain a natural rhythm synchronized with the cycles in the vegetable and mineral worlds. The poems gathered in *Second Sight* two decades later complicate our understanding of the processes in nature by invoking more impersonal and abstract 'cultural constructions' of time.

The refinement is most perceptible in a poem like 'Saturdays', which is a variation on the idea of 'the chronicle of a death foretold'. Addressing himself in a second person again, as he does in 'Looking for the Centre', Ramanujan imagines his own death occurring in Chicago, on

> a Saturday at three-fifteen
> at home in a foreign place
> where you jog,
> as gold needles of rain
> scatter the Art Fair in the park.

The exact day, place, and time are important because the poem explicitly responds to and rewrites Cesar Vallejo's 'Black Stone on a White Stone', in which the Peruvian poet projects his own death at nightfall on a Thursday in Paris. (Vallejo died in a hospital in that city in 1938, deliriously longing to be in Spain, which was still ravaged by civil war). In this context, 'Saturdays' invokes the poetic possibility that 'the body we know' is not just a natural clockwork mechanism but, more elaborately, 'an almanac'. As an almanac, the human body would be a record as well as forecast of astronomical events, lunar and solar cycles, high and low tides, agricultural activities, changes of weather and season, and daily sunrises and sunsets. But while a farmer's almanac is based on empirical observation, factual data, and rational prediction, the body's metaphorical almanac incorporates more 'irrational' modes of charting the processes and patterns in nature and time. Such modes of tracking phenomena include myth, ritual, and even superstition, which give time its human structure and content, as well as its meaning and utility.

The alternative modes of temporal organization enable the poet's persona to see that his 'daily dying body' ironically serves as 'the one good omen / in a calendar of ominous Saturdays'. In his own fictionalized biography a Saturday is ominous because his mother and one of his brothers supposedly passed away on that day of the week, though on different dates and in different places. In historical time a Saturday is ominous because the ancient Romans set it aside for their games of death at the Coliseum, from which Syrian Christians—his wife's ancestors—could escape only by migrating out of imperial Rome. Most obviously, in Indian folk-belief 'the day of Saturn' invites disaster more than any other day in the week, while in Western astrological time it is ominous because it exercises a dark planetary influence on people, making those who are born on it melancholy, sullen, or 'saturnine'. In a moment of ironic superstition and saturnine irony, the poet can imagine his own end as a 'good omen', since dying on a Saturday would have the force of a predestined or overdetermined event. In fact, he feels that his body's internal rhythm is already synchronized with this composite calendar because

> Saturdays ache
> in shoulder and thigh bone,
> dim is the Saturday gone
> but iridescent is the Saturday to come:
> the window, two cherry trees,
> Chicago's four November leaves,
> the sulphuric sky now a salmon pink,
> a wife's always clear face
> now dark with unspent
> panic, with no third eye, only a dent,
> the mark marriage leaves on a small forehead
> with ancestors in Syria, refugees

> from Roman Saturdays.

In the freeze-frame of the future projected by his own and others' pasts, he sees himself 'imprisoned in reverse / in the looking- / glass image of a posthumous twin', who is 'the older man in the sage / blue chair' who turns around 'to walk through the hole in the air', and whose body contains, co-ordinates, and interconnects all natural, historical, mythical, and astrological cycles.

The poems from the last five or six years of Ramanujan's life—which actually ended early on a Tuesday morning in an operating-room in Chicago—explore other aspects of real and imaginary clocks and calendars. The late poem 'Fog', included in *The Black Hen*, adopts an unusually austere style to contemplate the nature of movement and change, as they appear simultaneously in the body, the natural world, the world of objects made by human beings, and the human mind. 'Sonnet' reworks some of the ideas and images of 'Fog' to create a more personal reflection on temporality, emphasizing the aspects of time that are neither remote and objective, nor fixed and abstract. The poem argues lyrically that movement is precisely what breaks down the boundaries we habitually impose between interior and exterior, proximity and distance, mind and body, or subject and object:

> Time moves in and out of me
> a stream of sound, a breeze,
> an electric current that seeks
> the ground, liquids that transpire
>
> through my veins, stems and leaves
> towards the skies to make fog and mist
> around the trees. Mornings brown
> into evenings before I turn around
>
> in the day. Postage stamps, words
> of unwritten letters complete with commas,
> misplaced leases and passports, excuses
> and blame swirl through the night
>
> and take me far away from home
> as time moves in and out of me.

Both 'Fog' and 'Sonnet' suggest that time is woven into the very fabric of the body that is intermeshed with the co-extensive webs we call 'nature' and 'culture'. Temporality therefore manifests itself in human consciousness in several domains simultaneously: in the daily bodily experience of morning and night, in the clockwork rhythm of personal relationships and external seasons, and in the mind's foreknowledge of death.

A series of other poems in *The Black Hen* draws out the implications of this conception, bringing us closer to a social world embedded in history. 'At Zero', for example, unearths clocks—and their peculiar combination of rhythmic movement and eerie stillness—inside every kind of object and being on earth. Inanimate, dead, or still living, these range surreally from clock-towers, airplanes poised for take-off, and spinning potters' wheels to brahman widows, pulsing doves, and the scrotums of dead bulls. In contrast, 'August' experiments with the notion that the annual calendar, which is constructed empirically and rationally, can be recast as the cyclical chronology of the anniversaries of the births, deaths, quarrels, marriages, and divorces in the history of one extended family. That is, an objective measure of time can be replaced by and become indistinguishable from a completely subjective accounting of days, months, and years. Complementing both 'At Zero' and 'August', 'Birthdays' projects birth and death as polar opposites in several concomitant temporal orders, ranging from bodily time, personal chronology, and family history to the clockwork in the perpetual-motion machine of nature.

'Foundlings in the Yukon', one of Ramanujan's striking last poems, enlarges this way of mapping the mutual interdependences of body, nature, culture, and time until they cover an immense span of human and natural history. The poem revolves around an actual incident in the Yukon Territory in northern Canada, one of the coldest inhabited regions on earth, where a group of miners discovered some seeds 'sealed off by a landslide / in Pleistocene times'. When planted, six of the seeds, which must have been in deep-freeze hibernation for at least ten thousand years, 'took root / within forty-eight hours / and sprouted / a candelabra of eight small leaves'. Like 'upstarts', the saplings that emerged from the seeds

> drank up sun
> and unfurled early
> with the crocuses of March
> as if long deep
> burial had made them hasty

for birth and season, for names,
genes, for passing on . . .

these new aborigines biding
their time
for the miner's night-light

to bring them their dawn,
these infants compact with age,
older than the oldest
things alive, having skipped
a million falls
and the registry of tree-rings,
suddenly younger
by an accident of flowering

than all their timely descendants.

The long movement from 'Towards Simplicity' and 'Death and the Good Citizen' to poems like 'Saturdays', 'At Zero', and 'Foundlings in the Yukon'—which takes us from the clock inside the human body to the earth's elemental clock—strongly questions the common modern assumption that time is linear. As the poems approach human and natural processes from various angles, they uncover forms of repetition, cyclical departure and return, as well as continuity and disruption that dismantle the whole scientific and technocratic myth of progressive temporality.

3

The extension of biological time to geological time symptomatically links Ramanujan's interests in time, culture, nature, and the body with his general interests in human history and society. Poems ranging from 'Saturdays' in *Second Sight* to 'Foundlings in the Yukon' in *The Black Hen* focus on the more abstract, impersonal, and even trans-human aspects of temporality and historical process, but they remain inextricable from a humanistic conception of the past and the present. From this viewpoint, history can be imagined and narrated only by a human subject, and only in relation to itself and to other human subjects, precisely those who constitute the 'raw material and victims' of historical events. Thus 'Bosnia'—probably the last complete poem Ramanujan wrote—questions war, death, tragedy, and contemporary history from a position of empathy with human subjects and victims, whether through the feelings of guilt and horror or of compassion and tenderness. Such an engagement with history arises from an interest in the concrete particulars of character, action, and situation in the past and the present, and specifically in their warm-blooded human origins and meanings.

Ramanujan's conception of history as a process with human subjects, who are almost always anti-heroic, is most directly articulated in several kinds of historical poems in *Relations* (1971). 'The Last of the Princes', for instance, satirizes characters who are social types rather than unique individuals, and whose interrelated life-stories can be narrated as a compressed, anti-romantic social history of a specific class of Indians (that of the rajas and maharajas, who were often romanticized during the Raj). The third section of 'Some Indian Uses of History on a Rainy Day' moves away from the kind of social history condensed in 'The Last of the Princes', and offers us a portrait of an easily recognizable psychological (rather than social) type, together with a diagnosis of a common kind of cross-cultural misunderstanding in history—in this case, a misrecognition caused by the so-called Aryan connection between Hindu India and Nazi Germany. Against the first two examples, 'History' explicitly uses a fictional account of family life to dramatize the general interdependence of observing subject and observed event in the constitution of historical knowledge.

In contrast to these three poems and the paradigms of historical understanding they represent, 'Small-scale Reflections on a Great House' is a circumspect contemplation of general historical processes and patterns. This poem offers us an ironic yet celebratory profile of a large Hindu extended family, tracing its history thematically (rather than chronologically) from about the end of the nineteenth century to the third quarter of the twentieth. The poem evocatively reflects on the customs, rituals, myths, and superstitions that are part of the family's everyday life; the permutations and combinations in which character-traits are transmitted over several generations; the upbringing of children and the shaping of several kinds of adult lives; the private and public facets of the family in a web of social trans-actions; and the series of minor and major tragedies that strike individual members and affect the whole household. Besides,the poem also alludes satirically to the colonial economy of the Raj, and symbolically re-enacts the family's transition from a tradi-tional Indian world to a distinctly more modern one over the period of a century. As it gathers a large number of concrete details and symbolic particulars into its contemplative structure, 'Small-scale Reflections on a Great House' deliberately avoids turning into a family chronicle. Instead, it uncovers suggestive parallels between the family's fortunes and the modern social history of middle-class and upper-caste India as a whole, and hence acquires the shape of a national allegory. According to the allegorical argument of the poem, in the house that resembles the nation, 'nothing that comes in ever goes out'; everything inside circulates and recirculates over long periods of time; and despite the clutter and the confusion, nothing ever gets lost. That is, the economy of both household and nation is governed by a complete balance of means and ends, or what metaphorically might be called the 'law' of the material and moral 'conservation of energy'. Coloured by the ambiguities, paradoxes, and ironies that are typical of Ramanujan's social poetry, this poem paints one of the most memorable 'national portraits' of modern India that we have in twentieth-century poetry.

Ramanujan's poetic treatment of historical themes parallels and foreshadows his treatment of contemporary society and the individual self. We can interpret his social and personal poetry coherently if we assume that the human drama which constitutes the central dynamic of the past also serves as the mechanism that keeps the present-day world constantly in motion. This drama comes sharply into focus if we rearrange the social and personal poems hypothetically within a series of concentric circles, in which the outermost periphery contains repre-sentations of various environments that lie on the edge of the poet's experience, while the innermost periphery brings together poems about the things that are closest to him. If we move inwards from the outer circle, we first encounter Ramanujan's more impersonal social poems, which often enact a drama involving nameless character-types, whom he perceives or imagines at a distance (e.g., 'If Eyes Can See' in *The Black Hen*). In the second circle, we come across more personal poems about the extended family, which contains not only uncles, aunts, and cousins, but also dead grandparents and great-grandparents as well as unborn grandchildren and great-grandchildren, all clustered synchronically and diachronically around the poet, his parents, and his siblings (e.g., 'The Hindoo: He Doesn't Hurt a Fly or a Spider Either' and 'Real Estate' in *Relations*). In the third zone, nested inside the sprawling extended family, we find representations of the ongoing everyday drama of the nuclear family, where the main characters are a husband, a wife, a daughter, and a son (e.g., 'Routine Day Sonnet' in *Relations* and 'Moulting' in *Second Sight*). In the fourth, still smaller, and more intimate circle located inside the nuclear family, we discover poems about love and marriage, in which the primary play revolves around a man and a woman, a pair of lovers, or a husband and a wife (e.g., the love poems to a wife in *Relations* and *Second Sight*, and the series on love in *The Black Hen*). In the fifth and smallest circle, which is compressed almost to a point, we come face to face with the poet by himself, as the individual who experiences everything, confronts himself more closely than anything else, and serves as the subjective centre which gives all the concentric zones of experience their basic structure and meaning (e.g., 'Conventions of Despair' and 'One Reads' in *The Striders* and 'Pain: Trying to Find a Metaphor' in *The Black Hen*).

If we provisionally arrange the poems in such a sequence for interpretive purposes, we notice that the extended family and the immediate family, together with the institution of marriage that stands at their common core, define a composite domestic sphere. From the reader's standpoint, this sphere resembles the 'interior landscape' of classical Tamil poetry in board outline, and mediates any relationship between an individual and the larger social world. The importance of the domestic sphere as a mediating factor may indicate why family life serves as a primary theme in many of Ramanujan's early poems, and as the main metaphor for society even in his later work. It may also suggest why the composite sphere of the family turns out to be a part of society that can potentially contain the whole, the web of domestic relations can function as the means to mapping and interpreting social relations in general. It may further explain why even his more intimate poems about marriage, parenthood, love, and himself cannot be merely autobiographical or confessional: like the poems on public themes that can be placed in the outer circle of experience, they seem to be part of a poetic vision in which self and society can be related to each other only through the networks of home and family.

But even while the domestic sphere emerges as the central 'metonymic metaphor' for society and as the principal stage for the drama of contemporary society, it remains deeply ambiguous. On the one hand, poems like 'Still Another for Mother' in *The Striders*, 'Love Poem to a Wife, 1' in *Relations*, and 'Son to Father to Son' and 'Looking and Finding' in *Second Sight* suggest that the domain of marriage and kinship is a theatre of unresolvable conflicts, betrayals, and ironic reversals. On the other hand, poems like 'Love Poem for a Wife, 2' and 'Entries for a Catalogue of Fears' in *Relations*, 'Extended Family' and 'Highway Stripper' in *Second Sight*, and 'August', 'Not Knowing', and 'Contraries' in *The Black Hen* depict the individual's responses to family-situations as a series of mixed feelings. Ramanujan's domestic poetry thus appears to articulate a sceptical vision of marriage and family over a period of three decades, undermining the centrality of the domestic sphere itself. Late poems like 'Bosnia', 'Shadows', and 'A Report' then translate this vision metonymically into an ironic and tragic vision of society and history.

4

One of the darker ironies of this vision of history and society is that the self, which stands at the centre of concrete experience, seeks constantly to escape from the domestic sphere because home seems like a prison-house of relations. As Ramanujan puts it in his translation of a classical Tamil poem in the *akam* genre, which serves as the epigraph to *Relations*.

> Like a hunted deer
> on the wide white
> salt land,
>
>> a flayed hide
>> turned inside out,
>
> one may run,
> escape.
>
>> But living
> among relations
> binds the feet.

If we find ourselves trapped in such a situation, we may be able to escape from it if we can find a principle or quality of transcendence in the individual self. But the self that desires freedom turns out to be entirely immanent: it is besieged by precisely the same contradictory forces that threaten to dislodge the domestic and social edifice built around it, and hence cannot be a source of autonomous power. 'Self-portrait', the poem in *The Striders* with which Ramanujan usually began his public readings, identifies this problem precisely when it suggests that the self is more an absence than a presence in private as well as public space:

> I resemble everyone
> but myself, and sometimes see
> in shop-windows,
>> despite the well-known laws
>> of optics,
> the portrait of a stranger,
> date unknown,
> often signed in a corner
> by my father.

Moreover, even if we extract the self somehow from its network of human relations, we still cannot define it except in relation to things other than itself. This may explain why in 'Elements of Composition', the opening poem in *Second Sight*, the poet argues that he is composed, 'like others, / of elements on certain well-known lists', a matrix framed by 'father's seed and mother's egg' that is constantly

> gathering earth, air, fire, mostly
>   water, into a mulberry mass,
> moulding calcium,
>
> carbon, even gold, magnesium and such,
>   into a chattering self tangled
> in love and work . . .

These material substances, which are metaphorical in the poem, may seem to compose a person with determinate qualities, but the self passes 'through them / as they pass through' it, 'taking and leaving' everything from 'affection, seeds, skeletons' to the 'body-prints of mayflies' and 'millennia of fossil records / of insects that do not last / a day'. What is particularly paradoxical and ironic about the constitution of the self, in relation to its various 'others', is that the process which accumulates its defining characteristics becomes indistinguishable from the process which evacuates its identity. Ramanujan complicates this irony when he goes on to say that, 'even as I add',

> I lose, decompose
> into my elements,
>
> into other names and forms,
>   past, and passing, tenses
> without time,
>
> caterpillar on a leaf, eating,
>   being eaten.

When composition cannot be separated from decomposition, the self can possess a stable 'centre' or a principle of self-determined identity only in an ironic sense. So 'Looking for the Centre' in *Second Sight* refers satirically to the self as a perpetually 'missing' centre, because it evaporates the moment it seems to have been precipitated:

> Looking for the centre these days
>   is like looking for the Center
> for Missing Children
>
> which used to be here, but now has moved
>   downtown to a new building, southwest
> of the Loop,
>
> Kitty corner from the Second Chicago
>   Movers, last room to the left on the fifth
> floor. Ask there
>
> for the Center, anyone will tell you.

Finally, if the elusive self can be pinned down in spite of its transience, it turns out to contain multiple levels of consciousness or an infinite regress of identities. Following the Mundaka Upanishad among other sources, 'The Watchers' (also in *Second Sight*) speculates that the multiple layers of consciousness are like a group of disengaged observers housed in the body and the mind, who remain 'Lighter than light', blow 'like air / through keyholes', 'watch without questions', and 'watch even the questions'. Besides, 'They impose nothing, take no positions':

>   Unwitting witnesses,
> impotence
>
>   their supreme virtue, they move only
> their eyes, and all things seem to find their form.
>   Mere seers,
>
> they make the scene.

That is, at the end of the search for the self—which serves as the subjective centre of experience in the human and natural worlds, even as it seeks to escape from the web of domestic and social relations into a realm of independence—we find a series of 'mere seers' without substantial unity, agency, or will. These watchers can 'make the scene', in the double sense of the phrase, only by returning subjectivity to the objects, events, and relations it encounters routinely in its world of concrete particulars. As the self executes this paradoxical return, it locks itself into the space it wishes to leave in the first place: it involutes the entire historical and social structure, so that the innermost circle of experience elastically joins the outermost rim in the series of concentric circles, completing a loop from which there is no escape.

5

Ramanujan's poetry is like a circular labyrinth, in which all paths lead back to the point from where we start, no matter where we begin: the body in nature embodies natural time, which is the clock ticking inside history, which in turn is the clockwork mechanism inside a society that is paradoxically contained by its most prototypical part, the extended family, at the centre of which stands the self, housed in a real and imagined body. But this seemingly closed system, in which everything appears to be connected to everything else, does not come to us neatly encapsulated in such a form in his poetry, and hence cannot be an integrated 'system'. As 'Connect!' in *Second Sight* indicates, the imagination involved in composing poems is a 'disconnecting madness', which actively resists the call to perceive cycles in the processes of nature and culture, to link up 'black holes / and white noise' and 'red eclipses // and the statistics of rape', or to connect 'beasts with monks, slave economies / and the golden bough'. When this madness insists on disconnecting one concrete particular from another, and each particular from the general process or pattern it supposedly manifests, the poet's innermost 'watchers' remain silent spectators, as if 'they knew [that] my truth is in fragments'. The imagination composes by relating one thing to another, but it also breaks its own compositions into pieces.

This intricate double movement in Ramanujan's work, between 'stitching and unstitching', building and dismantling, or constructing wholes and producing fragments, became a little clearer to me one afternoon in Chicago, towards the middle of 1985. In the course of a casual conversation, he showed me the draft of a poem called 'Elements of Composition', which was then a single, long poem of a few hundred lines arranged in about twenty-five sections. It was a meditation on what we call the 'nature' of self and poetry, interspersed at various points with passages reflecting on certain 'epiphanic' moments in his life. I thought that it was a major poem with the sort of thematic scope, stylistic novelty, and imaginative impact that no Indian-English poet had been able to achieve until then. But Ramanujan was sure that his readers would misread it if he published it as it stood, because they would look in it for traces of earlier poems of a similar kind, from Wordsworth's *The Prelude* to Eliot's *Four Quartets*. He also felt strongly that the formal and thematic unity asserted by the long poem contradicted one of his central insights in it, that his own 'truth is in fragments'.

When he prepared the final manuscript of *Second Sight*, Ramanujan broke up the poem into fourteen relatively short poems. He subdivided some of the pieces further into sections and arranged all of them in similar-looking tercets, which gave them an unmistakable family-resemblance even when they were interspersed throughout the book with older, more recent, and rather different kinds of poems. In the seven years between the publication of *Second Sight* and his death, however, most readers seemed to miss the fact that 'Elements of Composition', 'Questions', 'The Watchers', 'Snakes and Ladders', 'A Poor Man's Riches' 1 and 2, 'Aliens', 'Drafts', 'Middle Age', 'The Difference', 'Dancers in Hospital', 'Connect!', 'Looking for the Centre', and 'Waterfalls in a Bank' belong to a single poetic design. Ramanujan must have been disappointed by this lack of discernment, and at certain moments may even have questioned his decision to disband the long poem. But so far as I know, he never went back to the unified version of 'Elements of Composition', in private or in print.

Ramanujan's refusal to accept merely conventional measures of coherence was a part of his search for a different kind of integrity. In his poetry, this integrity injects a unique urgency into his negotiations between body and mind, nature and culture, and history and contemporaneity. It also results in the constant, unpredictable movement of his poems in which structure articulates content, but connection thrives on disconnection; nature contains the body, but the body also contains nature; and the microcosm mirrors the macrocosm, but the whole finds its truest form in the fragment. Like his final vision of love, war, and death in 'Bosnia', his essential, life-long ideal of integrity could only be ironic.

Norman, Oklahoma
February-August 1994

I would like to thank Molly Daniels-Ramanujan and Krittika Ramanujan for reading several drafts of the Introduction; Michelle Stie for help with manuscript-preparation and proof-reading; the University of Oklahoma and its Department of English for generous support; and Aparna Dharwadker for criticism and patience at a difficult time.

Book One

The Striders (1966)

The Striders

And search
for certain thin-
stemmed, bubble-eyed water bugs.
See them perch
on dry capillary legs
weightless
on the ripple skin
of a stream.

No, not only prophets
walk on water. This bug sits
on a landslide of lights
and drowns eye-
deep
into its tiny strip
of sky.

'Strider' is the New England name for the water insect in this poem.

3

Snakes

No, it does not happen
when I walk through the woods.
But, walking in museums of quartz
or the aisles of bookstacks,
looking at their geometry
without curves
and the layers of transparency
that make them opaque,
dwelling on the yellower vein
in the yellow amber
or touching a book that has gold
on its spine,
                    I think of snakes.

The twirls of their hisses
rise like the tiny dust-cones on slow-noon roads
winding through the farmers' feet.
Black lorgnettes are etched on their hoods,
ridiculous, alien, like some terrible aunt,
a crest among tiles and scales
that moult with the darkening half
of every moon.

A basketful of ritual cobras
comes into the tame little house,
their brown-wheat glisten ringed with ripples.
They lick the room with their bodies, curves
uncurling, writing a sibilant alphabet of panic
on my floor. Mother gives them milk
in saucers. She watches them suck
and bare the black-line design
etched on the brass of the saucer.

The snakeman wreathes their writhing
round his neck
for father's smiling
money. But I scream.

Sister ties her braids
with a knot of tassel.
But the weave of her knee-long braid has scales,
their gleaming held by a score of clean new pins.
I look till I see her hair again.
My night full of ghosts from a sadness
in a play, my left foot listens to my right footfall,
a clockwork clicking in the silence
within my walking.
                         The clickshod heel suddenly strikes
and slushes on a snake: I see him turn,
the green white of his belly
measured by bluish nodes, a water-bleached lotus stalk
plucked by a landsman hand. Yet panic rushes
my body to my feet, my spasms wring
and drain his fear and mine. I leave him sealed,
a flat-head whiteness on a stain.
                                        Now
frogs can hop upon this sausage rope,
flies in the sun will mob the look in his eyes,

and I can walk through the woods.

The Opposable Thumb

'One two three four five
five fingers to a hand'
    said the blind boy counting
    but he found a sixth one
    waiting like a cousin for a coin;
    a budlike node complete with nail,
    phalanx, and mole
under the usual casual opposable thumb.

'One two three four five
five fingerspans for a woman's blouse',
    said the muslin-weaver spanning
    but he found his span shorter by a thumb:
    a puckered stump, sewn like a sausage head
    by a barber, without a nail
    phalanx or rice-grain line,
instead of the usual casual opposable thumb.

Said my granny, rolling her elephant leg
like a log in a ruined mill:
    'One two three four five
    five princes in a forest
    each one different like the fingers on a hand',
    and we always looked to find on her paw
    just one finger left of five: a real thumb,
    no longer usual, casual, or opposable after her husband's
knifing temper one sunday morning half a century ago.

Breaded Fish

Specially for me, she had some breaded
fish; even thrust a blunt-headed
smelt into my mouth;

and looked hurt when I could
neither sit nor eat, as a hood
of memory like a coil on a heath

opened in my eyes: a dark half-naked
length of woman, dead
on the beach in a yard of cloth,

dry, rolled by the ebb, breaded
by the grained indifference of sand. I headed
for the shore, my heart beating in my mouth.

On a Delhi Sundial

Four-faced clocks on market-towers school the town
and make the four directions sell and buy
in the stalls below where watches run
their certainties on the uncertain pulse.
Pretty machines on mantels slice the country silence.
And all give up their four and twenty ghostly
circles on to time like rings
from a smoker's youth.

Only sundials today do not remind you
of the rings under your eyes. Their time's
circles never drive beyond the dusk
but lie down as children's hoops
beneath the shoe-infested stairs. Only they
sleep with us in the dark and wake into time
with the light of the moon like antiquity's
lovers.

But who, among tourists
on a five-day tour, can put the clock back
and run into sundial time?
Or endure these wheeling knives that mince
the night for the morning's breakfast?

A Leaky Tap After a Sister's Wedding

Drop after drop
falls from its slightly incontinent mouth

    like mallet touches
    of silversmiths nextdoor.
    Our sisters were of various sizes,
    one was ripe for a husband
    and we were not poor.

Every third note is duller
and the fourth is a note higher
than the others, resting, it seemed, for a
quarter-second.

    They often stopped: maybe for a chat
    with a buyer,
    or a dip
    into patchwork pouches for betelnut
    and tobacco,
    or likelier still, to lay
    a little silver nest-egg under the mat
    to hatch on a rainy day.

But no.
That was no silversmith nextdoor
working for my sister's wedding.

    It is a single summer woodpecker
    peck-peck-Peck-pecking away
    at that tree
    behind the kitchen.

My sister and I have always wished a tree
could shriek or at least writhe
like that other snake
we saw
under the beak
of the crow.

Two Styles in Love

I

Love, you are green only to grow yellow.
Circling sickles in the wind will reap
your ghost from the branching gallows.
You will need no help to get to the heap.

While behind them dragon-breaths are burning
in fairytales men manage to love. O sweet,
don't talk of growth, of gorilla-heads sunflower-turning
toward the almost-man. Youth's a sowing of shell-less nut.

Come, the blatant sky is breaking into frost.
Eunuch shine is on the rain. The hidden
dogstar sniffs at the peeping toms, and night will be sudden:
Your one face, found in a rush of nettles, will be lost.

II

Love, only green has a fall of yellow
hours. Only growing has gold to reap.
Shake out your tresses of starlit willows
and slowly my dawn will climb, a lover who shall not sleep.

Love is no hurry, love is no burning;
it is no fairytale of bitter and sweet.
Moons may turn at the full; we return without turning.
And no mouth shall have shadow for meat.

No, no love is sudden.
Coupling hands take time to kill the frost.
Even leaping Beast shall wait to be bidden
by Beauty. Come lightly, love, let us wait—to be found, to be
    lost.

Still Life

When she left me
after lunch, I read
for a while.
But I suddenly wanted
to look again
and I saw the half-eaten
sandwich,
bread,
lettuce and salami,
all carrying the shape
of her bite.

This Pair

the envy of the elegant
childless couple, and the virgin aunt,

this fertile shabby pair
faintly smell already of unwashed hair,

worry about cash
and that powder they use for diaper rash

on certain fundamental places.
They chatter of downtown faces,

movies, of tennis on the lawns,
sandalwood rooks and ivory pawns,

of books in windows, neon signs,
the happy walks in shoplit rains

they seem to have traded,
without any discount, for that Thing hardly kneaded

into human shape by some obstetric stranger,
filling with its rage the literal manger

of their youth among breathing cows
that have begun to look like nurses on their toes.

On the Very Possible Jaundice of an
Unborn Daughter

When mynahs scream in the cages
    siamese cats with black on their paws
    tiptoe from the sulphur mines of the sun
    into the shadow of our house.

Father sits with the sunflower at the window
    deep in the yellow of a revolving chair,
    fat, bilious, witty, drawing small ellipses
    in the revolving air.

And plunges in a parallax of several eclipses
    to our earth where we pull grasshoppers' wings
    and feed red ink and lemon-peel
    to dragonflies.

And if that daffodil too flaps all morning
    in grandma's hands, how can my daughter
    help those singing yellows
    in the whites of her eyes?

Still Another for Mother

And that woman
beside the wreckage van
on Hyde Park street: she will not let me rest
as I slowly cease to be the town's brown stranger and guest.

She had thick glasses on. Was large, buxom,
like some friend's mother. Wearing chintz
like all of them who live there, eating mints
on the day's verandahs.
                  And the handsome
short-limbed man with a five-finger patch of gray
laid on his widows' peak, turned and left her
as I walked at them out of the after-
glow of a whiskey sour. She stood there
as if nothing had happened yet (perhaps nothing did)
flickered at by the neons on the door,
the edges of her dress a fuzz, lit red.
Fumbled at keys, wishbone shadows on the catwalk,
as though they were not keys, but words after talk,
or even beads.
              He walked straight on, towards me,
beyond me, didn't stop at the clicks of red
on the signals.
              And she just stood
there, looking at his walking on, me
looking at her looking on. She wanted then
not to be absent perhaps on the scene
if he once so much as even thought
of looking back.
              Perhaps they had fought.
Worse still, perhaps they had not fought.

I discovered that mere walking was polite
and walked on, as if nothing had happened
to her, or to me:
                        something opened
in the past and I heard something shut
in the future, quietly,
                        like the heavy door
of my mother's black-pillared, nineteenth-century
silent house, given on her marriage day
to my father, for a dowry.

Lines to a Granny

Granny,
tell me again in the dark
about the wandering prince;
and his steed, with a neem-leaf mark
upon his brow, will prance
again to splash his noonday image
in the sleep of these pools. He will break
with sesame words
known only to the birds,
the cobweb curtained door; and wake
the sentinel, the bawdy cook;
the parrot in the cage
will shout his name
to the gossip of the kitchen's blowzy flame.

Let him, dear granny,
shape the darkness
and take again
the princess
whose breath would hardly strain
the spider's design.

But tell me now: was it for some irony
you have waited in death
to let me learn again what once you learnt in youth,
that this is no tale, but truth?

A Rather Foolish Sentiment

said of course to a girl sometime ago

I have no head for tunes,
so into the dark I can carry
no singing voices, no flutes;

no eye for colours either,
so no pigments for my cavemen painting,
nor even the gold and the silver
filaments
that lanterns are said to throw upon your hair;

but only the passing touch
of people whom I once touched
in passing when they let me
pass. Perhaps it will not pass,
for in that touch I think I stumbled
on a pulse, and wondered like a fool

who has no proper sense of body
if it were yours, or mine,
and wondered if you wondered too.

18

Looking for a Cousin on a Swing

When she was four or five
she sat on a village swing
and her cousin, six or seven,
sat himself against her;
with every lunge of the swing
she felt him
in the lunging pits
of her feeling;
                    and afterwards
we climbed a tree, she said,

not very tall, but full of leaves
like those of a figtree,

and we were very innocent
about it.

Now she looks for the swing
in cities with fifteen suburbs
and tries to be innocent
about it

not only on the crotch of a tree
that looked as if it would burst
under every leaf
into a brood of scarlet figs

if someone suddenly sneezed.

I Could Have Rested

I could have rested.
Had I the wrong word,
had I the courage
to be gawky and awkward,
I'd have breasted
my shotgun pulses
and spread my patchwork sail
between her smile
and the counter-image
of her twining love for someone else's
love. Had I been a coward,
had I been even cold
or just old and Paracelsus,
I could have rested now.
I would have sold
and fled my treeless island youth
and told her
several birds ago
before they nested
in the south
of my burning foolish mouth.

On Memory

Ask me:
nursery rhymes
on Tipu Sultan or Jack and Jill:
the cosmetic use of gold when
the Guptas ruled:
an item of costume in
Shakespearian times;

or about
an eagle blotch
on the wall of a one-day room;
and the feel of a diamond scratch
on an acquaintance's
wedding-ring; these, and such as these
will gabble away their

tangent
answers, like desperate
urchins from a village school. But not
for all my blood-beat
nor the drill of that woodpecker beak
my will,
can I hold or keep

one face
and those words random-thrown
in a tumble of your multiple faces
as they turn in this day's dazzle,
this sun-struck house of mirrors.
Memory,
in a crowd of memories, seems

to have no place
at all for unforgettable things.

Instead of a Farewell

To meet and say farewell
to this part of me
that turns and returns
with a different partner
in a square dance,
meeting before I begin to see,
seeing after I have done
with meeting,
squaring at last in a glimpse
the ancient circle
of you and me:

how can I say farewell
when farewells are made
only for people who stay
and only for people
who go away?

Self-Portrait

I resemble everyone
but myself, and sometimes see
in shop-windows,
    despite the well-known laws
    of optics,
the portrait of a stranger,
date unknown,
often signed in a corner
by my father.

The Rickshaw-Wallah

His arms and legs were wholly literate:
in green and in red,
the indelible
names of friends long-dead.

His chest had the three names
of one woman, and several incredible
forms, now gone in the teeth,
the bitches, their limbs

loosely strung like linen-dolls,
their breasts no longer the faces of lambs.
But he, he would take all comers yet,
especially the thin-stemmed witches.

The tattoo will stand, green, red,
when all else is gone, he said.

Which Reminds Me

I have known
that measly-looking man,
not very likeable, going to the bank
after the dentist,
catching a cold
at the turn of the street
sitting at the window of the local bus,
suddenly make
(between three crossings and the old
woman at the red light)
a poem.

Which reminds me
of the thrown-away seed
of the folktale tree
filling with child the mangy palace dog
under the window,
leaving the whole royal harem
barren.

Sometimes

every morning
is a morning after,

only night has a roof
and the day has weals

on her back, as if
she had slept on a rafter.

Chess Under Trees

with an ex-maharajah

The mountain skies
were preoccupied by dynasties
of the mountain-pine:

while their tattered banners
harped at the drizzling strings of rain,

you lost the queen, and I won—
forgetting my manners.

No Man Is an Island

The entire island:
an alligator
sleeping in a mask of stone.
A grin of land
even on good days; on bad,
the ocean foams in that mouth.

Certain small sea-birds are said
to pick its teeth
for yellow crabs and jelly-fish.

But this man,
I know, buys dental floss.

Anxiety

Not branchless as the fear tree,
it has naked roots and secret twigs.
Not geometric as the parabolas
of hope, it has loose ends
with a knot at the top
that's me.
         Not wakeful in its white-snake
glassy ways like the eloping gaiety of waters,
it drowses, viscous and fibered as pitch.

Flames have only lungs. Water is all eyes.
The earth has bone for muscle. And the air
is a flock of invisible pigeons.
                But anxiety
can find no metaphor to end it.

KMnO₄ in Grandfather's Shaving Glass

A drop of color,
the permanganate purple of daily strangeness,
plummets
into the meniscus
of a tall
watercolumn of clarity
lensing a scratch on the wall.

It descends,
slow-motioned by the element,
unravelled into a loosening skein
of unravelling strands
of looser vein,
tress,
and filament,

curving into the light
with the faintest current
of stillness: the sight
twined,
untwined, in this
analysis
by sheer descent,

till pallor
pales into transparency,
till it leaves again a watercolumn
of clarity
slightly blued
by a past sensation,

still lensing that scratch
on the wall: till another,
still another drop unpacks its knots
of darkness into the capillary roots
of colour, adding hue on hue
till water is brewed

to winedark.

Christmas

Here in dawn's routine
rectangle
my eastern window
frames a tree:
Euclid's ghost
arrest-
ing life for me.

Bare
with December,
open
and shut
as an angle,
a skinny Janus,
my tree is two in one.

But where I come from
things are timed
differently.
My window
sometimes seems quite cunning
in defining
all at once
the abstract skies
with a leftward
leap
of greens,
a shock of leaf
upon Christmas eyes.
And I am limed
on branches bare as roots,
with that latest
hatch of birth-bewildered
parrots.

For a moment, I no
longer know
leaf from parrot
or branch from root
nor, for that matter,
that tree
from you or me.

Conventions of Despair

Yes, I know all that. I should be modern.
Marry again. See strippers at the Tease.
Touch Africa. Go to the movies.

Impale a six-inch spider
under a lens. Join the Test-
ban, or become The Outsider.

Or pay to shake my fist
(or whatever-you-call-it) at a psychoanalyst.
And when I burn

I should smile, dry-eyed,
and nurse martinis like the Marginal Man.
But, sorry, I cannot unlearn

conventions of despair.
They have their pride.
I must seek and will find

my particular hell only in my hindu mind:
must translate and turn
till I blister and roast

for certain lives to come, 'eye-deep',
in those Boiling Crates of Oil; weep
iron tears for winning what I should have lost;

see Them with lidless eyes
saw precisely in two equal parts
(one of the sixty-four arts

they learn in That Place)
a once-beloved head
at the naked parting of her hair.

Must go to bed
with frog-eyed dragons,
once my dream-dark queens

when I had a cavalry of princeling sons.
And I must draw, ductile,
the sudden silver of a glimpse

through the hole of a stare
and see a grandchild bare
her teen-age flesh to the pimps

of ideal Tomorrow's crowfoot eyes
and the theory of a peacock-feathered future.
No, no, give me back my archaic despair:

It's not obsolete yet to live
in this many-lived lair
of fears, this flesh.

A Certain Democrat

The exclusiveness of such things as policemen's
hospitals and a game of marbles behind a fence
always got his goat.

He loved late-evening frogs for breaking up bridge-parties
in verandahs of rattan chairs. Cultivated a taste
for porcelain tiles

especially in stations where seventeen dirty milkmen
and a boy jump regularly on the train when
city colleges have their teas.

Hated that bland third cousin, the beast, living
with a fourth in exclusive sin, prancing to go places
in the most ancient east.

And the mere thought of white enamelled eyeballs on the
    faces
of lean black men, or the sight of tight green oranges
or the virginities

of tirupathi dolls and small waspish women
rushed all his gall and blood to his brain with their
loud cries for violation.

Towards Simplicity

Corpuscle, skin,
cell, and membrane,
each has its minute seasons
clocked within the bones.

Millions grow lean and fall away
in the hourly autumn of the body.
But fertile in fall, ending as others begin,
to the naïvete of death they run.

From the complexity
of reasons gyring within reasons,
of co-extensive spring and autumn,

into the soil as soil we come,
to find for a while a simplicity
in larger, external seasons.

A River

In Madurai,
              city of temples and poets
who sang of cities and temples:

every summer
a river dries to a trickle
in the sand,
baring the sand-ribs,
straw and women's hair
clogging the watergates
at the rusty bars
under the bridges with patches
of repair all over them,
the wet stones glistening like sleepy
crocodiles, the dry ones
shaven water-buffaloes lounging in the sun.

The poets sang only of the floods.

He was there for a day
when they had the floods.
People everywhere talked
of the inches rising,
of the precise number of cobbled steps
run over by the water, rising
on the bathing places,
and the way it carried off three village houses,
one pregnant woman
and a couple of cows
named Gopi and Brinda, as usual.

The new poets still quoted
the old poets, but no one spoke
in verse
of the pregnant woman
drowned, with perhaps twins in her,
kicking at blank walls
even before birth.

He said:
the river has water enough
to be poetic
about only once a year
and then
it carries away
in the first half-hour
three village houses,
a couple of cows
named Gopi and Brinda
and one pregnant woman
expecting identical twins
with no moles on their bodies,
with different-coloured diapers

to tell them apart.

A Hindu to His Body

Dear pursuing presence,
dear body: you brought me
curled in womb and memory.

Gave me fingers to clutch
at grace, at malice; and ruffle
someone else's hair; to fold a man's
shadow back on his world;
to hold in the dark of the eye
through a winter and a fear
the poise, the shape of a breast;
a pear's silence, in the calyx
and the noise of a childish fist.

You brought me: do not leave me
behind. When you leave all else,
my garrulous face, my unkissed
alien mind, when you muffle
and put away my pulse

to rise in the sap of trees
let me go with you and feel the weight
of honey-hives in my branching
and the burlap weave of weaver-birds
in my hair.

Excerpts from a Father's Wisdom

Despair

Just comb your hair.
You shouldn't worry about Despair.
Despair is a strange disease.
I think it happens even to trees.

Day and Night

Only the day is up-to-date,
Even in ancient times
night
was ancient.

Safety in Love

If you wish to be safe in love
court a mermaid.
She's single-thighed.

Sculpture

Only sculpture proves
that ghosts copulate
with stone
even when people are looking.

Suicide

A man committed suicide
with all his clothes on
in a city pond:
few people strip for death.

Heredity

Even Accident woos
only the accident-prone.
Even gambling dues
are bred in an ancestor's bone.

Everything

Everything seems naked these days.
Trees, the women who seem to come right through nylon
    sarees,
redbrick buildings with only collars of cement,
paperback books sold without jackets:
even qualities
walk nude like dogs and cows.

Warning

Poverty is not easy to bear.
The body is not easy to wear.
So beware, I say to my children
unborn, lest they choose to be born.

Epitaph on a Street Dog

On the hedges grew the low melon moons.
Before the crescent dark could sink her teeth
   our bitch had all her mangy suitors
      sparring for a wreath
       of the midnight noons
   in her womb. And they were no neuters.
She spawned in a hurry a score of pups,
all bald, blind, and growing old at her paps;
         some of them alive
enough to die in the cold of her love.

Peacocks may have eyes in their tails, and crests.
But She had in a row four pairs of breasts,
where blind mouths plucked and swilled their fill
till mouths had eyes, and She was full of flies.

Images

After Meeting a Celebrity

I will pass from his mind
as image from a mirror.

Then why was I so clever?

Some Days

Waking is a blow
of light;
and walking, a sleet
of faceless acquaintances.

Still Another View of Grace

I burned and burned. But one day I turned
and caught that thought
by the screams of her hair and said: 'Beware.
Do not follow a gentleman's morals

with that absurd determined air.
Find a priest. Find any beast in the wind
for a husband. He will give you a houseful
of legitimate sons. It is too late for sin,

even for treason. And I have no reason to know your kind.
Bred Brahmin among singers of shivering hymns
I shudder to the bone at hungers that roam the street
beyond the constable's beat.' But there She stood

upon that dusty road on a nightlit april mind
and gave me a look. Commandments crumbled
in my father's past. Her tumbled hair suddenly known
as silk in my angry hand, I shook a little

and took her, behind the laws of my land.

An Image for Politics

Once, I'd only heard
of a Chinese fancy-dish
of fish
that rots
till it comes alive
and a maggot-spaghetti squirms
where once a mackerel gasped for worms:

cannibal
devouring smaller cannibal
till only two equal
giants are left to struggle,
entwined,
like wrestlers on a cliff:

and at last
only One
omnipotent
maggot-ceasar who rent
his rival
and lived—
of all the mob and the triumvirate,
his fat and lonely body stiff
and blind with meat,
his wrings without a wriggle—

for a slit-eyed Chinaman
to pluck and serve on a not-too-clean
willow-pattern plate
to a lean
and curious tourist.

Case History

What had he done
to crush glass in his fist
one middle-aged morning, known

only as morning by clocks without the sun?
At seven, his slingshot had not hit
the frosted childhood's streetlight:

he was no looting horseback Hun
out of his history books. On
evenings full of bats' wings

he had scarcely seen a sister raped by a dead father's sin
but only shaped by a mother's word. In
the swirl of his teens he had perhaps thrilled

to raisin-thefts and one kiss under the stairs. Once he ran
from a body-house without windows
looking for the wombs of faceless women

he never filled
with sons. But now he has glass in his fist
and several rows

of futures that could not reach any past.

One Reads

Daily, and therefore calmly, one reads:
of the raving Ganges,
the boats overturned;
a summer's thatch of villages
most casually burned;
our night's pomegranate mines
that cast
their ember seeds
into the future and the changing past
of files, charts and last year's twins,
the once-tended hives
in the garden,
or even
the unwaiting sociable wives.

But through the tall headlines
one hears now and then
the ambushed silence:
the pebbled ebb of crested tides
where no one rides
upright:
the wildcat quiet
of evil in distant worlds,
the narrowing spiral of reeling birds
and bankrupt brood that hatch like lice
in other men's sunday suns.

Then, one sees
the leprosy of light and shade,
the sunlit beggar squatting
on his shadow, clotting
the antlers of bare April's trees:
pandering lies
for our charity's
counterfeit *pice.*

A *pice* is a small copper coin.

Lac into Seal
on a kind of politics

When summer months branch backward
day after day after day
you'll only see now and then
a crow or two stropping
its beak on the back of a cow.

But if you look you'll find
in the armpits of trees whole rows
of bead-eyed beetle laying
for days their bowels' designs.
But you'll never once suspect

that all these beetles dream endlessly
of futures and seals of state
and signatures of brass
on their most casual turd
or that they will ever begin

to open their mouths in public
to claim for their insect
bodies' tentative periodic
itch a taste for History
and the National Cause.

The Fall

Falling,
I think of a man falling,
a plummet in a parachute
that will take half his life to sprout and take root,
while he, a mere body, a surrender,
a will-less plunge into the downward
below his blindness, cannot find a word
for a curse, nor an eye for a hook.
Then
the sudden catch
of grace,
of finding that even face-
less men have fingers in a row;
and the slow, all-too-slow
unfurling
of help behind his back,
segment by segment, of a silk bowl
held upside down to hold the pouring howl
of a pack of winds,
a grip on the crotch
of his braces, a mothercat's teeth
on the scruff of her kitten,
the very air a sheath
of safety
for the floating, the amniotic floating without hands
into an exhilaration
of larks, a man
amassed for all the darks
now a-dangle
at the threads and spangles
of ecstasy.

The careful calculus
of the retarded fall draws
the earth-map under the lenses,
projects the trees, blanches
to a blur the contour lines
isolating the needle-pines
till he almost begins
to count,
till he reaches
his end, the Ground,
all his limbs but scratches
on the rubble,
misses by the mere limp of a foot
the flower behind the ear
of a prickly pear
in the violence of the dragging wind,
a fallen rider held by his reins
to a flight of horses.

He finds his feet.
Sparse, alien houses
watch.
Some windows
slam on a flash: fieldglasses
on a hill
without the tallness of a tree or the wideness
of a street.

A Poem on Particulars

In our city markets
I have often seen a wicker basket
sit
upon its single, ample
hip,
its rattan pattern filled
with another,
subtler
bubble-bed pattern of oranges:

pellmell piled,
not one with a stain,
some thick-painted green all over,
others
with just a finger-print
of green;
some so ripe, there was a hint
of fungi-ash
on a slightly hollowed cheek;
some flushed and saffron,
some gamboge, some tangerine;
some pulpy, velvet-skinned,
their inner fist
of fingers
held rather loosely, and each day
more loosely,
in their body's
grandpa grip.

But
every one of these
had an absurd, almost human
umbilicus
at the top
where once the Tree
had poured its
future
from forgotten roots
and possessed it close,
to feed
this Fall-minded
pot-bellied
bud
till it rounded
for our baskets.

I have heard it said
among planters:
you can sometimes count
every orange
on a tree
but never
all the trees
in a single
orange.

Book Two

Relations (1971)

Like a hunted deer
on the wide white
salt land,

a flayed hide
turned inside out,

one may run,
escape.

But living
among relations
binds the feet.

From a Classical Tamil Anthology
(1st–3rd century A.D.)

It Does not Follow, but When in the Street

yellow trees bend over broken glass
and the walls of Central Jail
drip with spring's laburnum
yellows, yellow on yellow,

I forget the eczema on my feet,
the two holes in my shoe: at once I know
I'll have a sharp and gentle daughter,
an old age somewhere; I walk on air,

I walk on water, can even bear
to walk on earth for my wife
and I will someday somehow share

a language, a fire, a clean first floor
with a hill in the window; and eat
on an ancient sandalwood door.

Man and Woman in Camera and Out

In the small bright square
of the viewfinder
one image slurs another.

I try to match the circle
with the square, play
at the hocuspocus

of man, tree, and door,
peeking in and out
of the black box

with left eye and right
eye and the eye in between,
screwing them high and low,

fingering the focus,
reading the obvious light
by digits, the blind

feeling the blind,
knowing light by heat
and a wall by the wind,

till by a tiny act
of grace multiples
jell to a duplicate,

half man, half tree,
the left above the right,
they slide to meet

in a symmetry
of two eyes in a face,
the circle in the square

no enlargement of nose
or liver, but lifesize, exact,
small as the rest of him,

brown man in dotted tie
and five o'clock shadow,
the cherry tree behind

in bloom, not loosened yet
as it would be tomorrow.
With a click of luck

I married him then,
married a focus, now
a photograph in a frame

on the table in my living room,
while he himself goes
in and out of sight,

smooth by morning,
hairy by night,
growing from blur

to focus and back.

A Wobbly Top

At times, the wobbly top father gave me
quietly, after we both had a tantrum,

suddenly begins to spin so fast it's still:
every scar on its body now describes

a perfect circle within other scars'
perfect concentric circles, as in

a time-exposure of the sky.

Of Mothers,
among other things

I smell upon this twisted
blackbone tree the silk and white
petal of my mother's youth.
From her ear-rings three diamonds

splash a handful of needles,
and I see my mother run back
from rain to the crying cradles.
The rains tack and sew

with broken thread the rags
of the tree-tasselled light.
But her hands are a wet eagle's
two black pink-crinkled feet,

one talon crippled in a garden-
trap set for a mouse. Her sarees
do not cling: they hang, loose
feather of a onetime wing.

My cold parchment tongue licks bark
in the mouth when I see her four
still sensible fingers slowly flex
to pick a grain of rice from the kitchen floor.

THE HINDOO: *he doesn't hurt a fly or*
a spider either

It's time I told you why
I'm so gentle, do not hurt a fly.

Why, I cannot hurt a spider
either, not even a black widow,

for who can tell Who's Who?
Can you? Maybe it's once again my

great swinging grandmother,
and that other (playing at

patience centered in his web)
my one true ancestor,

the fisherman lover who waylaid her
on the ropes in the Madras harbour,

took her often from behind
imprinting on her face and body

(not to speak of family tree
or gossip column)

lasting impressions of his net:
till, one day, spider-

fashion, she clamped down and bit
him while still inside her,

as if she'd teeth down there—
they'd a Latin name for it,

which didn't help the poor man one bit.

And who can say I do not bear,
as I do his name, the spirit

of Great Grandfather, that still man,
untimely witness, timeless eye,

perpetual outsider,
watching as only husbands will

a suspense of nets vibrate
under wife and enemy

with every move of hand or thigh:
watching, watching, like some

spider-lover a pair
of his Borneo specimens mate

in murder, make love with hate,
or simply stalk a local fly.

Time and Time Again

Or listen to the clocktowers
of any old well-managed city

beating their gongs round the clock, each slightly
off the others' time, deeper or lighter

in its bronze, beating out a different
sequence each half-hour, out of the accidents

of alloy, a maker's shaking hand
in Switzerland, or the mutual distances

commemorating a donor's whim,
the perennial feuds and seasonal alliance

of Hindu, Christian, and Muslim—
cut off sometimes by a change of wind,

a change of mind, or a siren
between the pieces of a backstreet quarrel.

One day you look up and see one of them
eyeless, silent, a zigzag sky showing

through the knocked-out clockwork, after a riot,
a peace-march time bomb, or a precise act

of nature in a night of lightnings.

Love Poem for a Wife, 1

Really what keeps us apart
at the end of years is unshared
childhood. You cannot, for instance,
meet my father. He is some years
dead. Neither can I meet yours:
he has lately lost his temper
and mellowed.

In the transverse midnight gossip
of cousins' reunions among
brandy fumes, cashews and the Absences
of grandparents, you suddenly grow
nostalgic for my past and I
envy you your village dog-ride
and the mythology

of the seven crazy aunts.
You begin to recognize me
as I pass from ghost to real
and back again in the albums
of family rumours, in brothers'
anecdotes of how noisily
father bathed,

slapping soap on his back;
find sources for a familiar
sheep-mouth look in a sepia wedding
picture of father in a turban,
mother standing on her bare
splayed feet, silver rings
on her second toes;

and reduce the entire career
of my recent unique self
to the compulsion of some high
sentence in His Smilesian diary.
And your father, gone irrevocable
in age, after changing everyday
your youth's evenings,

he will acknowledge the wickedness
of no reminiscence: no, not
the burning end of the cigarette
in the balcony, pacing
to and fro as you came to the gate,
late, after what you thought
was an innocent

date with a nice Muslim friend
who only hinted at touches.
Only two weeks ago, in Chicago,
you and brother James started
one of your old drag-out fights
about where the bathroom was
in the backyard,

north or south of the well
next to the jackfruit tree
in your father's father's house
in Aleppey. Sister-in-law
and I were blank cut-outs
fitted to our respective
slots in a room

really nowhere as the two of you
got down to the floor to draw
blueprints of a house from memory
on everything, from newspapers
to the backs of envelopes
and road-maps of the United States
that happened

to flap in the other room
in a midnight wind: you wagered heirlooms
and husband's earnings on what
the Uncle in Kuwait
would say about the Bathroom
and the Well, and the dying,
by now dead,

tree next to it. Probably
only the Egyptians had it right:
their kings had sisters for queens
to continue the incests
of childhood into marriage.
Or we should do as well-meaning
hindus did,

betroth us before birth,
forestalling separate horoscopes
and mothers' first periods,
and wed us in the oral cradle
and carry marriage back into
the namelessness of childhoods.

Routine Day Sonnet

For me a perfectly ordinary
day at the office, only a red lorry
past the window at two;
a sailor with a chest tattoo.

A walk before dark
with my daughter to mark
another cross on the papaya tree;
dinner, coffee, bedtime story

of dog, bone and shadow. A bullock cart
in an Eskimo dream. But I wake with a start
to hear my wife cry her heart

out as if from a crater
in hell: she hates me, I hate her,
I'm a filthy rat and a satyr.

Army Ants

The army ants not only make their houses but they are their house, for of
their own living bodies they form the whole complicated dwelling.
C. Judson Herrick, The Thinking Machine

Ancestors give them aristocratic tastes:
        separate apartments
        for the queen,
        colonies

        for the various castes,
        several nurseries
        for the abstract

        and the bean-eyed young,
        hung perhaps with tigerheads
        of red wild ants

for trophies, or for vitamins.

        Army ants build each builder
        for a brick, altar
        and martyr in one,

        or a tile on the floor,
        part of the prize decor
        for the bedroom

        of their most illustrious queen
        where slow males
        die young

or live older than death in nurseries of eggs.

       Extremists, true makers
       of made things, they have
       only themselves

       for bricks; knees for hinges; heads
       for the plinths of their rain-
       soaked Corinths;

       the rafter a chainmail of stares
       and the running
       runway

a crazy pavement of hands and feet.

       Not like the Great Wall of China
       cemented with slave
       and enemy

       and the favourite almost dead;
       the living, the young,
       are the brick

       and the mortar of this house
       without legend.
       And the work,

as they say, is the workman at last.

One, Two, Maybe Three,
Arguments against Suicide

1

Don't forget, dear departing saint:
you see red, you faint, at the sight
of blood. And there's always the danger
you may be understood, as never
    before, misconstrued by some
    casual stranger. Your bluebeard
    motives all over the toilet floor,
    only your lifelong good name will go
to hell: the rest of you, wrapped
in kitchen-cloth bandages, waits
in line, in a one-bulb lawcourt
with in-laws for lawyers; your poor heart
    pounds on hospital images,
    tetanus, the bluntness of knives,
    the corpse's nose-hair, and how awful
    if found dead in such yellowed underwear.

2

Better not attempt that suicide,
for you may find you've already died

and there's nothing left to kill.
Worse still, you may die formally

now, yet live on forever in spite
of what those doctors certify:

your self now a mere odourless soul,
a see-through man-shaped hole

in the air, a late lamenting ghost
looking in vain for an empty seat

71

at the full house of your posthumous
fame where you can see but not hear

the rain of applause, the jangle
of medals on the breast of your happy

unhappy widow. Though you're there
you wish you really were, wish the rain

or a touch of that intangible breast,
even that garden hose full blast

on the rosebush would quench the icy fire,
the love you hate, that burns, consumes, yet leaves

you whole.

3

Desire, bodiless, is endless.
Remember what the wise callous hindus

said when the love-god burned: keep your cool,
make for love's sake no noble gesture.

All symbol, no limbs, a nobody all soul,
O Kama, only you can have no use

for the *Kamasutra.*
                         Ashes have no posture.

One More After Reading Homer

any cassandra with some e s p
can see the smoke grow thick
between her and the city faces
but she cannot show the sceptic

the brands in the marketplace.
cats in the alley may watch
the Stranger and walk close
to his knee to arch the fur

on their backs and mimic
the strut of later centurions.
cats being cats will purr
at all sorts of occult things

including a faint tattoo
on a great big wooden horse
getting wet in the rain.
neither paris nor cassandra

but only incurious cat   I come
upon a half-burned shoulderblade
greening in a lake of dead alewives
among leftovers papercups and condoms.

I wonder if in chicago too
love indifference and hate
in some devious way relate
at all to deaths by fire.

Some Indian Uses of History on a Rainy Day

1

Madras,
          1965, and rain.
Head clerks from city banks
curse, batter, elbow
in vain the patchwork gangs
of coolies in their scramble
for the single seat
in the seventh bus:

they tell each other how
Old King Harsha's men
beat soft gongs
to stand a crowd of ten
thousand monks
in a queue, to give them
and the single visiting Chinaman
a hundred pieces of gold,
a pearl, and a length of cloth;

so, miss another bus, the eighth,
and begin to walk, for King Harsha's
monks had nothing but their own two feet.

2

Fulbright Indians, tiepins of ivory,
colour cameras for eyes, stand every July
in Egypt among camels,

faces pressed against the past
as against museum glass,
tongue tasting dust,

amazed at pyramidfuls
of mummies swathed in millennia
of Calicut muslin.

3

1935. Professor of Sanskrit
on cultural exchange;
                          passing through; lost
in Berlin rain; reduced
to a literal, turbanned child,
spelling German signs on door, bus, and shop,
trying to guess *go* from *stop*;
                          desperate
for a way of telling apart
a familiar street from a strange,
or east
from west at night,
the brown dog that barks
from the brown dog that doesn't,

memorizing a foreign paradigm
of lanterns, landmarks,
a gothic lotus on the iron gate;

suddenly comes home
in English, gesture, and Sanskrit,
assimilating
                the swastika
on the neighbour's arm
in that roaring bus from a grey
nowhere to a green.

A Lapse of Memory

As there are such things as the liar's
use of truth, and the well man's use
of illness, there must be an amnesiac

use of memory.
                    After the lightning
strikes the tree and takes all the leaves,
an amnesiac may break into hives

but recognize nothing present
to his concave eye groping only
for mother and absences. Nothing

at all is family now to that estrangement:
neither the squares of office, nor round wife,
nor oblong home address with two

initials and a lifelong name. Friends
and family doctors hope he'll recover
all pasts and circulation of sap

back into fingertips through one crack
or lapse of memory somewhere in the inverse
branching under the earth. Maybe all it takes

is the smell of a woman's perfume
in a childhood latrine, a peanut seller's
raucous cry, or three obscene lines

mating white and black lizards
in schoolbook Sanskrit. Or a slant
of rain on the sunshine and the papaya tree.

Eyes, Ears, Noses, and a Thing
about Touch

Eyes are fog,
are trees green or on fire,
a man's face quartered by the cross-
hairs of a gunsight. Crows, scarecrows,
eyes in others' eyes. A brown dog
dipped and gilded in the sunshine,
or blurred through someone else's glasses.

When lucky
it dawns birdcries,
the ear has children with bells;
the fall, delay, and fall
of a wooden doll on the wooden
stairs, what mother says
to cook and early beggar.

Urine on lily,
women's odours
in the theatre, a musk cat's
erection in the centre of a zoo,
the day's bought flowers
crushed into a wife's night
of grouses: the sudden happiness

of finding
where noses can go.
Touch alone has untouchables,
lives continent in its skin, so
segregating the body
even near is too far.
Through all things that press,

claw, draw blood,
yet do not touch,
it remembers a wet mouth
on a dry; clammy hands and tactless
manoeuvres on the ironwork
with the dew on the iron
in the two o'clock woods;

the burr I plucked
from your back's hollow,
the six, or eight, light
hairy legs of the tree spider
that walked the small of my back
and gave me a rash
for seven whole days.

THE HINDOO: *he reads his GITA and is calm at all events*

At this party heads have no noses, teeth close
upon my heart: yet I come unstuck
and stand apart. I do not marvel
when I see good and evil: I just walk

over the iridescence
of horsepiss after rain. Knives, bombs, scandal,
and cowdung fall on women in wedding lace:
I say nothing, I take care not to gloat.

I've learned to watch lovers without envy
as I'd watch in a bazaar lens
houseflies rub legs or kiss. I look at wounds calmly.

Yet when I meet on a little boy's face
the prehistoric yellow eyes of a goat
I choke, for ancient hands are at my throat.

Poona Train Window

I look out the window.

See a man defecating
between two rocks, and a crow.

Drink my railway tea.
A milestone newly
painted orange, black

numbers on its sides.
The blinding noise
and the afterhush
of one train passing

another, rise and fall
of hills in two sets
of windows, faces, a rush
of whole children, white
hair in a red turban.

I drink my railway tea.
Three women with baskets
on their heads, climbing
slowly against the slope
of a hill, one of them
lop-sided, balancing

between the slope and
the basket on the head
a late pregnancy.
Buffaloes swatting flies
with their tails.

Six gulls. The tea
darkens like a sick
traveller's urine.
Six gulls sitting still,

six eggs laid new
on grass, in, on, near,
water. I see a man

between two rocks.
I think of the symmetry

of human buttocks.

Time to Stop

There are times
           when
going to museums
makes you see

pointilliste anthills,

Picasso faces on milkmen
framed in the living room
window,

      a violet shadow
all around a dead
or dying cow
             and you come
back at night to see
how it looks
under the gaslight,

and after an accident,
                blood
looks remarkably
like fresh paint.

        Then
it's time to stop
going to museums.

After a night of rage
that lasted days,
quarrels in a forest,
waterfalls, exchanges, marriage,
exploration of bays
and places
we had never known
we would ever know,

my wife's always
changing syriac face,
chosen of all faces,
a pouting difficult child's
changing in the chameleon
emerald
wilderness of Kerala,
small cousin to tall

mythic men, rubberplant
and peppervine,
frocks with print patterns
copied locally
from the dotted
butterfly,
grandmother wearing white
day and night in a village

full of the colour schemes
of kraits and gartersnakes;
adolescent in Aden among stabbing
Arabs, betrayed and whipped
yet happy among ships
in harbour,
and the evacuees,
the borrowed earth

under the borrowed trees;
taught dry and wet,
hot and cold
by the monsoons then,
by the siroccos now
on copper
dustcones, the crater
townships in the volcanoes

of Aden:
           I dreamed one day
that face my own yet hers,
with my own nowhere
to be found; lost; cut
loose like my dragnet
past.
I woke up and groped,
turned on the realism

of the ceiling light,
found half a mirror
in the mountain cabin
fallen behind the dresser
to look at my face now
and the face
of her sleep, still asleep
and very syriac on the bed

behind: happy for once
at such loss of face,
whole in the ambivalence
of being halfwoman half-
man contained in a common
body,
androgynous as a god
balancing stillness in the middle

of a duel to make it dance:
soon to be myself, a man
unhappy in the morning
to be himself again,
the past still there,
a drying
net on the mountain,

in the morning, in the waking
my wife's face still fast
asleep, blessed as by
butterfly, snake, shiprope,
and grandmother's other
children,
by my only love's only
insatiable envy.

Entries for a Catalogue of Fears

1

Though I cannot always tell a fear
from a hope or a hope from a face
in the window
of a house on fire,
I know
fears far more precise
than any hope.
Born blind, a whole skin listening
and a seeing ear,
they do not have to grope.

2

Add now, at thirty-nine, to the old old fear
of depths and heights,
of father in the bedroom,
insects, iodine
in the eye,
sudden knives and urchin laughter
in the redlight alley,
add now
the men in line
behind my daughter.

3

My delicate
nails grow long
during a public lecture
and no one will hear me for
the noise of rustling nails nor
see my face
for the rivalry of their silicate
tangle.

4

I'll grow
charitable one day,
begin to classify
at dawn the week's breadcrumbs
in a plastic bag for the red and black
street ant,
the beggardoves in the park:
the free sapphire bluejay
in the tree
will make a habit
of the shelled peanut
in my hand.

5

Sixty, and one glass eye,
even I talk now and then of God,
find reasons to be fair
everywhere
to the even and to the odd,
see karma
in the fall of a tubercular sparrow,
in the newspaper deaths in Burma
of seventy-one men, women and children;
actually see the One in the Many,
losing a lifetime of double vision
with one small adjustment
of glasses.

6

Like any honest
man, unnerved by the slightest
inquiry into his flawless past,
found spotted all over with horrid fact
by the mere act
of questioning:
or found helplessly handling
my thing
at seventy
on a doorstep
wiping out a whole difficult lifetime
of dignity
and earning only the fascination
of passing
old women.

7

Not ceasing upon the midnight,
wakened by the heat
of abandoned crematory fires
or by vultures;

not being dead
as a tree under wood-
peckers plucking
out worms like nerves; with just enough
left to know

about vultures
and their unerring arts
of picking
on soft parts
like testicles and coconut brains.

8

I'll love my children
without end,
and do them infinite harm
staying on the roof,
a peeping-tom ghost
looking for all sorts of proof
for the presence of the past:

they'll serve a sentence
without any term
and know it only dimly
long afterwards
through borrowed words
and wrong analyses.

THE HINDOO: *the only risk*

Just to keep the heart's simple given beat
through a neighbour's striptease or a friend's suicide.
To keep one's hand away from the kitchen knife

through that returning weekly need
to maim oneself or carve up wife
and child. Always and everywhere, to eat

three square meals at regular hours; suppress
that itch to take a peek at the dead street-
dog before the scavengers come. Not to be caught

dead at sea, battle, riot, adultery or hate
nor between the rollers of a giant lathe. Yes,
to keep it cool when strangers' children hiss

as if they knew what none could know nor guess.
At the bottom of all this bottomless
enterprise to keep simple the heart's given beat,

the only risk is heartlessness.

Real Estate

My cousin knows buildings;
he knows them well.
He can even tell
their gender by one look
at the basement.
Architect of our vertical
future, man of vision with a perfect
eye for parallax, he has compasses
in his rods and cones.
                              Where he is
there are cranes in the sky, pigeons
in the not-yet plaza.
                              He always knew
glass was good. 'It's rational,
it reflects',
enlisting attitudes of sky,
cloud, dazzle, aeroplanes,
for the man in the street;
filters images of the sun's
eclipse for the passerby;
                              yet refracts
all things for the man within,
defining some men in, others out,
with apparent transparency.

Humanist, he calculates
stress and strain on wood
and steel, on liver and lower brain.
When the lift gets stuck
in the marble quarry
or workmen go berserk
on the thirtieth floor,
his men collect within the hour
for the widows and the clerk
who lost his head in that altitude.

Yet he cannot exclude
the indiscipline of the second look
at mushrooms after rain
in the children's rooms, those
yellow thumbs in the reeking
crotches of rotting timber
bought years ago
for my uncle's
very carefully imagined
houses.
         Only we, our uncle's nephews, know
windows without walls
or the kinds of grass that grow
in the twinkle of an uncle's eye.

Any Cow's Horn Can Do It

Mention any cousin's death
in the walled red-fort city:
she'll weep aloud with no thought
of neighbours.
        Any reminder
of her youth's market places
crawling with feeling hands, eyes
groping for the hidden hooks
that hold together little girls
and she will glow green fire
from all nine wells of a woman's
shame.
        She'll grow cold remembering
what is not forgotten:
getting belted by father
standing on a doorstep
with a long strip of cowhide
and the family idiom
the day he caught her
in the hotel lobby,
            mother's mouth
working red over betel leaf
and betelnut, the clove ground
into the nutmegs of satisfaction
seeing a disobedient daughter
brought to her senses.

Any old quarrel over novel,
movie, or a suspicion
of pregnancy is enough
to make wife, sister, or girl friend
walk silent from room to room
smouldering with no care for burned
rice or the black nails of children
before visitors; a soreness
on two granules of her throat

93

will do it.
        Any number of things
can make a woman lie awake
and watch window-squares crawl out,
grow oblong and vanish
all night long with every car
in the street till morning's small
shadowless hour.

Any cow's horn tilted at
a child in the street will do it,
but nothing you say with words
in a poem will make her scream,
get sick, or go grey in the face.
You'll never do it, for poems
cannot flay like eyes or hurt
like a fall on a sidewalk,
cannot replace the panic
runs for imaginary
children in the middle room
of a house with the porch
on fire. Poems aren't even words
enough to rankle, infect
or make the smallest incisions
unless wife, girl friend or sister—

and I'm not talking of strangers
or the unborn—
               somehow are
made to think it's all about
their shame in the market, or
an elegy on the death
of a far-off cousin.

When It Happens,

there will be surprises: mothers mean harm,
throw stepmother shadows on the woodwork.
Neither analysis, nor astrology

will help, but a virgin widow may bring
ripe papayas, a glass of pigeon's blood still warm,
a backdoor address in whorehouse alley.

Brothers practise circus knives, stand you between
identical alternative nightmares:
            wrench it out from its root in the belly,

            hook it out with a coat-hanger,
            flush it in the bathroom with *draino*
            like a careless pregnancy

            after a picnic with loafers. Yet you know
it has to be endured, be born head first,
licked into a likeness and a face,

every bit of the afterbirth eaten
before the strangers come with their compliments.
Or else a bulbous foetal eye

in formalin pickle will outstare
you from a schoolroom jar,
the twin vein on its sallow lid indigo

with age, when you Mother Superior go there
to give away prizes
to girlscouts and campfire girls.

Small-Scale Reflections on a Great House

Sometimes I think that nothing
that ever comes into this house
goes out. Things come in every day

to lose themselves among other things
lost long ago among
other things lost long ago;

lame wandering cows from nowhere
have been known to be tethered,
given a name, encouraged

to get pregnant in the broad daylight
of the street under the elders'
supervision, the girls hiding

behind windows with holes in them.

Unread library books
usually mature in two weeks
and begin to lay a row

of little eggs in the ledgers
for fines, as silverfish
in the old man's office room

breed dynasties among long legal words
in the succulence
of Victorian parchment.

Neighbours' dishes brought up
with the greasy sweets they made
all night the day before yesterday

for the wedding anniversary of a god,

never leave the house they enter,
like the servants, the phonographs,
the epilepsies in the blood,

sons-in-law who quite forget
their mothers, but stay to check
accounts or teach arithmetic to nieces,

or the women who come as wives
from houses open on one side
to rising suns, on another

to the setting, accustomed
to wait and to yield to monsoons
in the mountains' calendar

beating through the hanging banana leaves.

And also, anything that goes out
will come back, processed and often
with long bills attached,

like the hooped bales of cotton
shipped off to invisible Manchesters
and brought back milled and folded

for a price, cloth for our days'
middle-class loins, and muslin
for our richer nights. Letters mailed

have a way of finding their way back
with many re-directions to wrong
addresses and red ink marks

earned in Tiruvella and Sialkot.

And ideas behave like rumours,
once casually mentioned somewhere
they come back to the door as prodigies

born to prodigal fathers, with eyes
that vaguely look like our own,
like what Uncle said the other day:

that every Plotinus we read
is what some Alexander looted
between the malarial rivers.

A beggar once came with a violin
to croak out a prostitute song
that our voiceless cook sang

all the time in our backyard.

Nothing stays out: daughters
get married to short-lived idiots;
sons who run away come back

in grandchildren who recite Sanskrit
to approving old men, or bring
betelnuts for visiting uncles

who keep them gaping with
anecdotes of unseen fathers,
or to bring Ganges water

in a copper pot
for the last of the dying
ancestors' rattle in the throat.

And though many times from everywhere,

recently only twice:
once in nineteen-forty-three
from as far away as the Sahara,

half-gnawed by desert foxes,
and lately from somewhere
in the north, a nephew with stripes

on his shoulder was called
an incident on the border
and was brought back in plane

and train and military truck
even before the telegrams reached,
on a perfectly good

chatty afternoon.

Smalltown, South India

I return from the wide open spaces.
Temple employees have whiskered nipples.
The streetcows have trapezium faces.
Buffaloes shake off flies with a twitch of ripples.

I sink to the seabed in a barrel.
Water-layers salt and pickle the sun.
Toes mildew green, trees are porous coral:
ambush of city shark and wifely dolphin.

I bed down with long finless slipper fish.
The ceiling has weeds, the sleep is brackish.

100

Some Relations

1   *nursery turtles*

grounded here, carrying a daily cross
of window bars, an ordinary square
of sun, glowing and dimming with each cloud
up there:

      my daughter's turtles try
to hibernate in the jar, very far
from the ocean, beginning to be confused
by the heat of this Chicago winter

2   *kitten on tigerskin*

not yet fully recovered
from birth,
          blinking
blackwhite kitten yawn,
mew, make water
on a livingroom tigerskin
with green glass eyes
and shellac tongue

3   *a praying mantis*

a praying mantis, deathly still
on a yellow can of DDT
in the Madurai temple—

someone's cleaning out scorpions
from the many armpits of Shiva
one leg in the air

          broken by time
          or a passing Muslim
          from Ghazni

my finger grows a lizard face
your pubic hair is tornado grass

my daughter's daughter's unborn face
floats to the surface: it has the natural

piety of the praying mantis
after a kill, its own or a butterfly's—

all over me are greenish
soft underbellies of ancestral

crocodiles and tortoises
the silent thud of their bloodbeat

—yet I do not shudder
at the coldness of their blood

Take Care

In Chicago it blows
hot and cold. Trees
play fast and loose.
     Kittens and children
     have tics: the old
     have things in their
     eyes. So, do not breathe
deeply. Practise
analysis.
Invisible crabs
     scuttle the air.
     Small flies sit
     on aspirin and booze.
     Enemies have guns.
Friends have doubts.
Wives have lawyers.

Smudge your windows.
Draw the blinds.
All tall buildings
     use telescopes.
     Give daughters pills,
     learn karate.
     Prepare to get raped
bending for a book.
Go to the opera
in brown overalls,
     wear pure plastic
     on the daily bus.
     Think of the stink-
     bomb in the barber's
chair. Expect the knife
on the museum stair.

When you are there
take special care
not to stare
    at peppergrinders,
    salt shakers, or the box
    of matches on the black
and white squares
of your kitchen cloth.
They take on the look
of meat grinders,
    cement shakers,
    boxes against boxes
    in the grilled
    city: intersections
of wet black splinter,
of houses burned

in the white oblongs
of winter, three T-
squares standing
    for the backstairs,
    the blacks black
    as the blacks
    in the Christmas snow
or the statistics
of City Hall
and Skid Row.
    In Chicago,
    do not walk slow.
    Find no time
    to stand and stare.
Down there, blacks look black.
And whites, they look blacker.

The Last of the Princes

They took their time to die, this dynasty
falling in slow motion from Aurangzeb's time:
some of bone TB,
others of a London fog that went to their heads,

some of current trends, imported wine and women,
one or two heroic in war or poverty,
with ballads
to their name. Father, uncles, seven

folklore brothers, sister so young so lovely
that snakes loved her and hung dead,
ancestral
lovers, from her ceiling; brother's many

wives, their unborn stillborn babies, numberless
cousins, royal mynahs and parrots
in the harem:
everyone died, to pass into his slow

conversation. He lives on, heir to long
fingers, faces in paintings, and a belief
in auspicious
snakes in the skylight: he lives on, to cough,

remember and sneeze, a balance of phlegm
and bile, alternating loose bowels and hard
sheep's pellets.
Two girls, Honey and Bunny, go to school

on half fees. Wife, heirloom pearl in her nose-ring,
pregnant again. His first son, trainee
in telegraphy,
has telegraphed thrice already for money.

Old Indian Belief

You need some

million ants with brief
methodical lives and calcium
limbs to build one ant-hill

and leave it in time
for the great recurring pattern
of the sudden snake.

No ant, red, white, or black,
can stand the smell
of a live cobra.

But they'll pick
the flesh off dead ones
to the last ivory rib:

with a little help
from rain, sun, and the natural
chemistry of recent flesh, they'll

leave snake skeletons
complete with fang and grin
for a schoolgirl's picnic

horror, and the local museum
collection of local celebrities.

History,

which usually
changes slowly,
changes sometimes
during a single conversation:

the petite little aunt
in her garden of sweet limes
now carries a different
face, not merely older or colder
or made holy
by deaths and children's failures.

For instance

the day my great-aunt died
I was there by one of those
chances children never miss,
looking for a green ball
I never lost. I saw her
laid out, face incurious
eyes yet unshut,
between glass curio bureaus
under a naked cobweb bulb
next to a yellow dim window.

And my little dark aunt was there
—nose eyes and knee-bend cut
fresh from stone for a Parvati statue—
looking for something, half
her body under the cot,
maybe a rolling pin
her little son had brought for play
from under the kitchen mob
of cooking and washing relatives.

                                    But yesterday
my mother said, I've never told
anyone what happened
that day your great-aunt died:
with all those children in and out
of the death-room, all the kith and kin
milling in the kitchen, wet faggot smoke,
and rumours about the will,
                                              her two
daughters, one dark one fair,
unknown each to the other
alternately picked their mother's body clean
before it was cold
or the eyes were shut,
        of diamond ear-rings,
        bangles, anklets, the pin
        in her hair,
        the toe-rings from her wedding
        the previous century,
        all except the gold
        in her teeth and the silver g-string
        they didn't know she wore
        her napkins on
        to the great disgust
        of the orthodox widows
        who washed her body
        at the end,

and the dark
stone face of my little aunt
acquired some expression
at last.

Compensations

I've even heard of surviving
World War men with wooden legs
doing cha cha cha's and jitterbugs
at Army Hospitals, near debris
and craters, especially
outside the amputation theatres;

the dumb and the colourblind rise
rapidly in politics; the born deaf
practise psychiatry as if
to the practice born; fingerless
men become tailors for royalty,
painters, filigree workers in

silver, or excel at the javelin
throw; with a hook for a hand
men hold and pull black strings
in a puppetshow or a boxing
syndicate; stutterers become salesmen
for things like machine guns

or pet woodpeckers; good
upstanding men deformed
by literacy abroad
return middle-aged to farming
and the innocence of knowing
a spade for a spade and a bird

for a bird, learning without
the benefit of names and forms
the works and the days, the signs
of fevers, madness and the rains:
miracles of vengeful reversal
like some spinsters' need to succeed

only as hydraulic engineers
in swarming barren lands, or the great
familiar men falling apart in state,
holding together, entire,
the ancient chaos of a country
by barely living on in a high chair

that ought to have wheels, renewing
honesty by their cunning, reviving
failing youth by just dying
at the wrong time, at the aimless
hand of an assassin, at the mercy
of a watch that ran too fast—

surpassed only by the last
miracle of grace, the three-eyed
whirlwind of arms, dancing on
a single leg though he can dance
on many, kind returning god
of Indian deluges,

dying from time to time
of sheer fatigue, leaving
the technicalities of war,
famine, riot and the rest
to us, two-handed two-legged normal us,
in a periodic transfer of powers.

Obituary

Father, when he passed on,
left dust
on a table full of papers,
left debts and daughters,
a bedwetting grandson
named by the toss
of a coin after him,

a house that leaned
slowly through our growing
years on a bent coconut
tree in the yard.
Being the burning type,
he burned properly
at the cremation

as before, easily
and at both ends,
left his eye coins
in the ashes that didn't
look one bit different,
several spinal discs, rough,
some burned to coal, for sons

to pick gingerly
and throw as the priest
said, facing east
where three rivers met
near the railway station;
no longstanding headstone
with his full name and two dates

to hold in their parentheses
everything he didn't quite
manage to do himself,
like his caesarian birth
in a brahmin ghetto
and his death by heart-
failure in the fruit market.

But someone told me
he got two lines
in an inside column
of a Madras newspaper
sold by the kilo
exactly four weeks later
to streethawkers

who sell it in turn
to the small groceries
where I buy salt,
coriander,
and jaggery
in newspaper cones
that I usually read

for fun, and lately
in the hope of finding
these obituary lines.
And he left us
a changed mother
and more than
one annual ritual.

Prayers to Lord Murugan*

1

Lord of new arrivals
lovers and rivals:
arrive
at once with cockfight and banner-
dance till on this and the next three
hills

women's hands and the garlands
on the chests of men will turn like
chariotwheels

O where are the cockscombs and where
the beaks glinting with new knives
at crossroads

when will orange banners burn
among blue trumpet flowers and the shade
of trees

waiting for lightnings?

2

Twelve etched arrowheads
for eyes and six unforeseen
faces, and you were not
embarrassed.

Unlike other gods
you found work
for every face,
and made

---

* Ancient Dravidian god of fertility, joy, youth, beauty, war, and love. He
is represented as a six-faced god with twelve hands.

eyes at only one
woman. And your arms
are like faces with proper
· names.

                        3

Lord of green
growing things, give us
a hand

in our fight
with the fruit fly.
Tell us,

will the red flower ever
come to the branches
of the blueprint

city?

                        4

Lord of great changes and small
cells: exchange our painted grey
pottery

for iron copper the leap of stone horses
our yellow grass and lily seed
for rams'

flesh and scarlet rice for the carnivals
on rivers O dawn of nightmare virgins
bring us

your white-haired witches who wear
three colours even in sleep.

                        114

5

Lord of the spoor of the tigress,
outside our town hyenas
and civet cats live
on the kills of leopards
and tigers

too weak to finish what's begun.
Rajahs stand in photographs
over ninefoot silken tigresses
that sycophants have shot.
Sleeping under country fans

hearts are worm cans
turning over continually
for the great shadows
of fish in the open
waters.

We eat legends and leavings,
remember the ivory, the apes,
the peacocks we sent in the Bible
to Solomon, the medicines for smallpox,
the similes

for muslin: wavering snakeskins,
a cloud of steam.
Ever-rehearsing astronauts,
we purify and return
our urine

to the circling body
and burn our faeces
for fuel to reach the moon
through the sky behind
the navel.

Master of red bloodstains,
our blood is brown;
our collars white.

Other lives and sixty-
four rumoured arts
tingle,

pins and needles
at amputees' fingertips
in phantom muscle.

7

Lord of the twelve right hands
why are we your mirror men
with the two left hands

capable only of casting
reflections? Lord
of faces,

find us the face
we lost early
this morning.

8

Lord of headlines,
help us read
the small print.

Lord of the sixth sense,
give us back
our five senses.

Lord of solutions,
teach us to dissolve
and not to drown.

9

Deliver us O presence
from proxies
and absences

from sanskrit and the mythologies
of night and the several
roundtable mornings

of London and return
the future to what
it was.

10

Lord, return us.
Bring us back
to a litter

of six new pigs in a slum
and a sudden quarter
of harvest.

Lord of the last-born
give us
birth.

11

Lord of lost travellers,
find us. Hunt us
down.

Lord of answers,
cure us at once
of prayers.

Book Three

Second Sight (1986)

Elements of Composition

Composed as I am, like others,
   of elements on certain well-known lists,
father's seed and mother's egg

gathering earth, air, fire, mostly
   water, into a mulberry mass,
moulding calcium,

carbon, even gold, magnesium and such,
   into a chattering self tangled
in love and work,

scary dreams, capable of eyes that can see,
   only by moving constantly,
the constancy of things

like Stonehenge or cherry trees;

add uncle's eleven fingers
   making shadow-plays of rajas
and cats, hissing,

becoming fingers again, the look
   of panic on sister's face
an hour before

her wedding, a dated newspaper map
   of a place one has never seen, maybe
no longer there

after the riots, downtown Nairobi,
   that a friend carried in his passport
as others would

a woman's picture in their wallets;

add the lepers of Madurai,
    male, female, married,
with children,

lion faces, crabs for claws,
    clotted on their shadows
under the stone-eyed

goddesses of dance, mere pillars,
    moving as nothing on earth
can move—

I pass through them
    as they pass through me
taking and leaving

affections, seeds, skeletons,

millennia of fossil records
    of insects that do not last
a day,

body-prints of mayflies,
    a legend half-heard
in a train

of the half-man searching
    for an ever-fleeing
other half

through Muharram tigers,
    hyacinths in crocodile waters,
and the sweet

twisted lives of epileptic saints,

and even as I add,
I lose, decompose
into my elements,

into other names and forms,
past, and passing, tenses
without time,

caterpillar on a leaf, eating,
being eaten.

Ecology

The day after the first rain,
for years, I would come home
in a rage,

for I could see from a mile away
our three Red Champak trees
had done it again,

had burst into flower and given Mother
her first blinding migraine
of the season

with their street-long heavy-hung
yellow pollen fog of a fragrance
no wind could sift,

no door could shut out from our black-
pillared house whose walls had ears
and eyes,

scales, smells, bone-creaks, nightly
visiting voices, and were porous
like us,

but Mother, flashing her temper
like her mother's twisted silver,
grandchildren's knickers

wet as the cold pack on her head,
would not let us cut down
a flowering tree

almost as old as her, seeded,
she said, by a passing bird's
providential droppings

to give her gods and her daughters
and daughters' daughters basketfuls
of annual flower

and for one line of cousins
a dower of migraines in season.

No Amnesiac King

One knows by now one is no amnesiac
king, whatever mother may say or child believe.

One cannot wait any more in the back
of one's mind for that conspiracy

of three fishermen and a palace cook
to bring, dressed in cardamom and clove,

the one well-timed memorable fish,
so one can cut straight with the royal knife

to the ring waiting in the belly,
and recover at one stroke all lost memory,

make up for the years drained in cocktail glasses
among dry women and pickled men, and give back

body to shadows, and undo the curse
that comes on the boat with love.

       Or so it seems,

as I wait for my wife and watch the traffic
in seaside marketplaces and catch

my breath at the flat-metal beauty of whole pomfret,
round staring eyes and scales of silver

in the fisherman's pulsing basket,
and will not ask, for I know I cannot,

which, if any, in its deadwhite belly
has an uncooked signet ring and a forest

legend of wandering king and waiting
innocent, complete with fawn under tree

and inverse images in the water
of a stream that runs as if it doesn't.

In the Zoo
a tour with comments

And these
these are scavenger birds
                        fit emblems
for a city like Calcutta
or Madurai
crammed to the top of its gates

They are known generally
as adjutant storks
                        yes they have a long-legged dignity
that's slightly vulgar

Adjutant storks come in three shades
a faded black
                        like Madras lawyers *a grey*
a dirty white
                        like grandmother's maggoty curds

They are rather noisy and heavy
in their take-off
and flap themselves into air
                        like father
into the rain, his baggy umbrellas with three ribs
broken by his sons in a fencing match and three
by last year's winds

But once air-borne
                        this furry spider-legged auntie
of a bird
            it circles
on motionless wings

128

                    filling the sky's transparency
with slow sleepy perfect circles
like father's Magic Carpet story
that rowdy day when the rainstorm leaked
through the roof
and mother was ill
and he had to mop
the kitchen of our pattering feet

Questions

Two birds on the selfsame tree:
one of them eats the fruit of the tree,
the other watches without eating.
                    Mundaka 3.1.1

1

Eating, being eaten,
    parts of me watch, parts of me burn,
rarely a clear blue flame

without a sputtering of questions:
    why now, why here, why the Down's
syndrome

in the genes of happiness,
    the dead twin's cord of birth
noosed

around his brother's neck,
    a favourite dog eating puppies
in the garden,

why the fall into bliss on a cloudy afternoon?

2

Under the grey rains of June,
    in the black patience of stone elephants,
were the watchers there

with me, being born over and over, tearing
    each time through a waterbed paradise,
the original ocean

of milk, gills for lungs, the whole body
    a sucking at the nipple, a past perfect
of two in one,

130

my head's soft crown bathed in mother's blood,
    wearing tatters of attachments, bursting
into the cruelties

of earthly light, infected air?

Fear

For you, fear
is Terror,

wound museums
of Hiroshima,

the smell
of cooking

in Dacca sewers,
Madame Nhu's

Buddhist barbecues;
that well-known child

in napalm flames
with X-ray bones

running, running,
a stationary march

in the rods
and cones

of everyone's
Reuter eyes.

My fear,
small,

is a certain knock
on the backdoor

a minute
after midnight,

132

thirty years ago
or anytime now;

or a tiny
white lizard,

its stare, deadsnake
mouth,

and dinosaur
toes,

flattened to a fossil
in the crease

of my monkey cap
by my rolling,

sleeping, ignorant
skull.

Astronomer

Sky-man in a manhole
with astronomy for dream,
astrology for nightmare;

fat man full of proverbs,
the language of lean years,
living in square after

almanac square
prefiguring the day
of windfall and landslide

through a calculus
of good hours,
clutching at the tear

in his birthday shirt
as at a hole
in his mildewed horoscope,

squinting at the parallax
of black planets,
his Tiger, his Hare

moving in Sanskrit zodiacs,
forever troubled
by the fractions, the kidneys

in his Tamil flesh,
his body the Great Bear
dipping for the honey,

the woman-smell
in the small curly hair
down there.

Death and the Good Citizen

I know, you told me,
    your nightsoil and all
your city's, goes still
    warm every morning
in a government
    lorry, drippy (you said)
but punctual, by special
    arrangement to the municipal
gardens to make the grass
    grow tall for the cows
in the village, the rhino
    in the zoo: and the oranges
plump and glow, till
    they are a preternatural
orange.

Good animal yet perfect
    citizen, you, you are
biodegradable, you do
    return to nature: you will
your body to the nearest
    hospital, changing death into small
change and spare parts;
    dismantling, not de-
composing like the rest
    of us. Eyes in an eye bank
to blink some day for a stranger's
    brain, wait like mummy wheat
in the singular company
    of single eyes, pickled,
absolute.

Hearts,
        with your kind of temper,
    may even take, make connection
with alien veins, and continue
    your struggle to be naturalized:
beat, and learn to miss a beat
    in a foreign body.
                        But
you know my tribe, incarnate
    unbelievers in bodies,
they'll speak proverbs, contest
    my will, against such degradation.
Hidebound, even worms cannot
    have me: they'll cremate
me in Sanskrit and sandalwood,
    have me sterilized
to a scatter of ash.

                        Or abroad,
they'll lay me out in a funeral
    parlour, embalm me in pesticide,
bury me in a steel trap, lock
    me out of nature
till I'm oxidized by left-
    over air, withered by my own
vapours into grin and bone.
    My tissue will never graft,
will never know newsprint,
    never grow in a culture,
or be mould and compost
    for jasmine, eggplant
and the unearthly perfection
    of municipal oranges.

The Watchers

1

Lighter than light, blowing like air
   through keyholes, they watch without questions,
the watchers,

   they watch even the questions, as I live
over and over with cancelled stamps,
   in verandas,

Poonas, bus burnings, Chicagos
   near a backyard well of India
smells, basements,

   small back rooms, upstairs, downstairs,
once even under the stairs
   on election day,

with a dog who groaned human in his sleep
   and barked at spiders.

2

They impose nothing, take no positions.
   It's the mark of superior beings,
says the Book

   of Changes, they can watch a game of chess
silently. Or, for that matter,
   a Chinese wall

cemented with the bonemeal of friends
   and enemies. Unwitting witnesses,
impotence

   their supreme virtue, they move only
their eyes, and all things seem to find their form.
   Mere seers,

they make the scenc.

Snakes and Ladders

Losing everytime I win, climbing
   ladders, falling to the bottom with snakes,
I make scenes:

in my anger, I smash all transparent
   things, crystal, glass panes, one-way mirrors,
and my glasses,

blinding myself, I hit my head on white
   walls, shut myself up in the bathroom,
toying with razors,

till I see blood on my thumb, when I
   black out, a child again in a glass booth
elevator, plummeting

to the earth five floors a second,
   taking my sky, turning cloud, and San Francisco
down to the ground,

where, sick to my stomach, I wake
   wide open, hugging the white toilet bowl,
my cool porcelain sister.

Pleasure

A naked Jaina monk
ravaged by spring
fever, the vigour

of long celibacy
lusting now as never before
for the reek and sight

of mango bud, now tight, now

loosening into petal,
stamen, and butterfly,
his several mouths

thirsting for breast,
buttock, smells of finger,
long hair, short hair,

the wet of places never dry,

skin roused even by
whips, self touching self,
all philosophy slimed

by its own saliva,
cool Ganges turning
sensual on him,

smeared his own private

untouchable Jaina
body with honey
thick and slow as pitch,

and stood continent
at last on an anthill
of red fire ants, crying

his old formulaic cry

at every twinge,
'Pleasure, Pleasure,
Great Pleasure!'—

no longer a formula
in the million mouths
of pleasure-in-pain

as the ants climb, tattooing

him, limb by limb,
and covet his body,
once naked, once even intangible.

A Poor Man's Riches 1

Winter is inventory time
    for toilet bowls in the hardware store;
in medical schools,

    for the hundred muscles you move
to stand perfectly still; in offices
    of immigration,

for coloured and discoloured aliens, brown
    eyes, father's name, five moles
classified

    in each oblong of visa and passport,
with only the pink, yellow, and green
    of a mango

from Acapulco to change the colours
    of poverty under the sweating
boiler pipes.

On the Death of a Poem

Images consult
one
another,

a conscience-
stricken
jury,

and come
slowly
to a sentence.

A Poor Man's Riches 2

Yet in April, between the lines
   of classified ads, it's spring,
dogwood blows white

   under a blight of elms, haiku
butterflies sleep in the ear
   of a ruined Buddha,

and we steal kisses, committing grand
   larceny under the boiler pipes
and I discover

   at last how a woman is made
as she laughs and makes a man
   of me,

teaches me combinations, how to pick
   locks to raid her richest furs,
and loot the mint

   of gold and silver even as they turn
into common money, leaving
   mouth marks,

lowtide smells, and fingerprints
   for all to see
in the secret accounts of joy.

A Minor Sacrifice

(remembering the dead in My Lai 4)

i

I'd just heard that day
of the mischievous king in the epic
who kills a snake in the forest
and thinks it would be such fun
to garland a sage's neck
with the cold dead thing,
and so he does,
and promptly earns a curse,
an early death by snakebite.

His son vows vengeance
and performs a sacrifice,
a magic rite
that draws every snake from everywhere,
till snakes of every stripe
begin to fall
through the blazing air
into his altar fires.

Then that day, Uncle, of all people,
a man who shudders at silk,
for he loves the worm,
who would never hurt a fly
but catch it most gently
to look at it eye to eye
and let it go,

suddenly strikes our first summer scorpion
on the wall next to Gopu's bed
with the ivory dragonhead
of his walking stick
and shows us the ripe
yellow poison-bead
behind the sting.

Grandmother then, tut-tutting
like a lizard,
tells us how a pregnant scorpion
will look for a warm secret place,
say, a little girl's underwear
or a little boy's jockstrap,
and then will burst her back
to let loose in her death
a host of baby scorpions.

'They're quite red at birth,
the little ones', Uncle says.
'They glow like hand-carved rubies
from Peking, redder than garnet,
especially when you hold them up
to the light.
And when they grow big,
they take on the colour of gray
China jade. Beautiful, beautiful',
he says, shaking his marmoset head.

                    ii
That afternoon, Shivanna asks me
under the sighing neem tree,
'Wouldn't you like to rid the world
of scorpions, if you could?'

'Yes, but how?'
            'Witchcraft', says he,
shining darker than an ebony turtle.
'We can make them come at our bidding
when the sun is in Scorpio,
like guests to a wedding,
into the bole of this very tree.
And they will burn in a bonfire
you and I will light.'

'What, all of them?'
'Yes, and every kind. Black, red,
white, yellow, young, old,
the three-legged and the blind.'

'Can we do it now?'
                    'Not so fast, kiddo.
What can you get without a sacrifice?
First, we've to feed
the twelve-handed god of scorpions
something he loves as other gods
love goats and rice.
For that you need
one hundred live grasshoppers
caught on a newmoon Tuesday.
But remember: no wings on those things.
Catch them next Tuesday,
and I'll show you twigs on this tree
that will drip with scorpion legs.'

'Will you come with me?'
                    'No', he says.
'I'm busy. Take Gopu with you.
You'll need three jars.'

iii

So we steal three pickle jars at dawn
on that breezy newmoon Tuesday.
Leaping and hopping all over the lawn,

we become expert by noon
at the common art
of catching grasshoppers on the wing,

learning by the way
to tell apart
twigs and twiglike insects

146

that turn slowly round the twigs,
shamming dead
at the touch of a mere look,

as if it could burn.

We unlearn
what we couldn't have in years,
some small old fears

of other living things,
though we're still squeamish
when we pull off their wings

and shiver a bit
as we put away
those wriggles in our bottles.

And we learn,
as from no book,
the difficult art of counting

little writhing objects
through glass walls
with flaws and bubbles.

They had tiny compasses for thighs,
and moviestar goggles
for eyes.

iv

By evening we have ninety-nine.
The hardest is the last,
maybe because they too are learning.

But Gopu, who knows by heart the score
of every Test Match,
stalks and pounces in the half dark.

147

Breathless, he almost crushes his catch.
So we make our century,
sneak by the backdoor

to the bath house
to scrub and scour with coconut fibre
till the skins of our palms come off.

That night we don't eat or sleep too well.
We draw sticks and it falls to Gopu's lot
to keep the jars of grasshopper cripples safe

under his bed
and even that savage innocent
dreams all night

of every punishment
in the narrow woodcut columns
of the yellowing almanacs of Hindu hells.

v

When we go to see Shivanna
on Wednesday morning,
the jars behind our backs,
most of the grasshoppers
rather still or very slow,

Shivanna's mother tells us
he is in the hospital
taken sick with some strange
twitching disease.
We never see him alive again.

Uncle says, later,
                'Did you know, that Shivanna,
he clawed and kicked the air
all that day, that newmoon Tuesday,
like some bug
on its back?'

148

Alien

A foetus in an acrobat's womb,
   ignorant yet of barbed wire
and dotted lines,

hanger-on in terror of the fall
   while the mother-world turns somersaults,
whirling on the single bar,

as her body shapes under water
   a fish with gills into a baby
with a face

getting ready to make faces,
   and hands that will soon feel the powder touch
of monarch butterflies,

the tin and silver of nickel and dime,
   and learn right and left to staple, fold
and mutilate

a paper world in search of identity cards.

Saturdays

Enter a five-cornered room.
See yourself as another,
an older face in the sage
blue chair, the whole room
turning a page:
white words in black stone,
you know without knowing how
death will fog
a Saturday at three-fifteen
at home in a foreign place
where you jog,
as gold needles of rain
scatter the Art Fair in the park.

Not on Thursday, not in Paris
at nightfall,
not in a local train as you'd like
but on a day like this,
three weeks into a garbage strike,
a Dutch elm dying against a redbrick wall
that you'll remember but not know why
looking into a sawtooth
sky in a sequoia forest.
The two fingers you learned to pop
on your sixth birthday
crook and ache now,
like mother's on her sixtieth.
She died in the kidney wing, hallucinating.

A brother's briar pipe chatters
between his teeth,
as his heart comes to a stop,
accepting failure
that first Saturday in April,
mouth filled with bile
in a green-walled hotel room
within earshot of the Bombay sea
after a meeting under a slow ceiling
fan, red tea, letters
melting in alphabet soup
in the Reserve Bank,
his last thoughts like coils of brown rope
down his village well, sand, rope of sand.

The body we know is an almanac.
Saturdays ache
in shoulder bone and thigh bone,
dim is the Saturday gone
but iridescent
is the Saturday to come:
the window, two cherry trees,
Chicago's four November leaves,
the sulphuric sky now a salmon pink,
a wife's always clear face
now dark with unspent
panic, with no third eye, only a dent,
the mark marriage leaves on a small forehead
with ancestors in Syria, refugees

from Roman Saturdays.
The kettle's copper, mottled with water spots,
whistles in the kitchen. You
stir and leave the five-cornered room,
left foot wronged in a right-foot shoe,
imprisoned in reverse
in the looking-
glass image of a posthumous twin.

Turn around
and see the older man in the sage
blue chair turn around
to walk through the hole in the air,
his daily dying body
the one good omen
in a calendar of ominous Saturdays.

Zoo Gardens Revisited

Once flamingoes reminded me of long-legged aunts in white cottons, and black-faced monkeys of grave lowbrow uncles with movable scalps and wrinkled long black hands. Now animals remind me only of animals,

orangutans of only orangutans, and of tuberculosis in the Delhi Zoo. And the symmetric giraffe in London that split in two trying to mount a coy female who gave him no quarter.

Visitors no longer gape at ostriches, so they tell me, but shrewdly set their tail feathers on fire with lighter fluid and cigarette lighters. So ostriches in zoos no longer hide their heads in sand as they do in proverbs.

Some, they say, feed bananas to the dying race of ring-tailed monkeys, bananas with small exquisite needles in them. So monkeys in zoos no longer eat bananas as they still do in temple cities and Jungle Books.

Tigresses, I hear, go barren, or superintended by curious officials adulterate their line with half-hearted lions to breed experimental ligers and tions as they breed pomatoes and totatoes in botanical gardens.

Eight-foot tigers yawn away their potency. Till yesterday, they burned bright in the forests of the night. It was a way of living. Now their eyes are embers in the ash. A slight movement of the eyelash flicks the ash.

The other day in Mysore a chimp named Subbu was paralysed neck down. He couldn't lift his chipped blue enamel mug to his lips and slurp his tea any more nor pout his lips to puff at his cigar.

The Society of Animal Lovers babysat for Subbu in shifts till in the small hours of the third morning he bit the sweetest lady of them all in a fury his protectors could not understand.

Lord of lion face, boar snout, and fish eyes, killer of killer cranes, shepherd of rampant elephants, devour my lambs, devour them whole, save them in the zoo garden ark of your belly.

Son to Father to Son

i

I am five,
I too dream of father,
   his beard a hanging hive,
turning slowly in his bed.
I scream at the hair
   on his hands
as they hold me close
to ask me why.

Sister swinging high
on the creaky swings,
   a window full of bees,
I could not tell him
his toes were talons,
   curving long
and slow
towards my sleep.

ii

It is no dream
to see a son skewered
   by a bamboo arrow
in a jungle trap;
or a daughter lowered
   like a match
into a sulphur mine
of hungry men.

I wake with a round
shadow for my head,
   the ceiling a falling
omen. A son's tall body
stands target at the door
   to ask me why
I keep so still and low.
How can I tell him

I see him shot,
washed, eyes shut,
   laid out,
I hear his cradle rock,
watch his ten little toes
   accuse my ceiling?

Drafts

1

A rough draft, getting rougher:
    a struggle in the crowd to see
the well-known

but half-seen Hyde Park rapist's face,
    half-seen perhaps only by another,
unseen

because seen too often; now towards,
    now away from what one thought
one always knew

without the help of policemen's
    drawings, a trayful of noses
and cruel lips.

2

Itself a copy of lost events,
    the original is nowhere, of which things,
even these hands,

seem but copies, garbled by a ciphered
    script, opaque as the Indus,
to be refigured

from broken seals, headless bodies,
    mere fingers, of merchants and dancers
in a charred city

with sewers, bath houses, a horned god
    of beasts among real homebodies,
family quarrels,

itches, clogs in the drain, the latter
  too ordinary to be figured
in the classic seals.

3

And we have originals, clay tigers
  that aboriginals drown after each small-
pox ritual,

or dinosaur smells, that leave no copies;
  and copies with displaced originals
like these words,

adopted daughters researching parents
  through maiden names in changing languages,
telephone books,

and familiar grins in railway stations.

4

The DNA leaves copies in me and mine
  of grandfather's violins, and programmes
of much older music;

the epilepsies go to an uncle
  to fill him with hymns and twitches,
bypassing me for now;

mother's migraines translate, I guess,
  into allergies, a fear of black cats,
and a daughter's passion

for bitter gourd and Dostoevsky;
  mother's almond eyes mix with my wife's
ancestral hazel

to give my son green flecks in a painter's eye,
  but the troubled look is all his own.

At Forty,

our Jatti, palace wrestler of Mysore,

teacher at the gym, has the grey
eyes of a cat, a yellow moustache,
and a whorl of tabby hair
on his chest.

No shirts under his military pea-coat
except on special days, when he wears
ribbons, medals and stripes—his father's
from World War One.

Someone in the palace is said to have said
one day, 'Jatti, the Wrestler, our teacher at the gym,
is now in top form, our state's very best',
and so they trim

his hair, give him all-body shaves to bring out
the fury of his yellow moustache.
Eggs and meat for breakfast, massages
of iguana fat,

till he glows in the dark, a lit medallion
figure. No sex, they whisper, for even
a look at your wife or that rumoured Muslim mistress
will drain

your power, loosen your grip. They weigh him,
measure his chest, his belly, his thigh,
and they pat his treasure. One April day,
they take him out

in a procession of purple turbans,
urchins, and burnished brass, the raucous
palace band on hire, from clocktower
to market square

to the white ropes of the red arena
in the Town Hall, where he is thrown
round after round, rolled over, jeered at
by rowdies

and sat upon by a nobody from nowhere,
a black hulk with a vulgar tiger's name
strutting in pink satin shorts. Jatti,
the Wrestler,

our teacher at the gym, walks away,
shaking off a swarm of eyes and hands, walks fast
and slow, in white trunks and bare feet,
through backstreet mats

of drying grain, straight to the gym,
to the red earth pit where he'd sparred
all year. Neck-deep he buries his body
in familiar ground,

only his bloodshot eyes moving in his head
and sometimes his short-haired scalp,
tabby-grey; his moustache unwaxed, turned down,
caked with mud.

Five disciples, we fumble and exercise
under a dusty bulb with dumb-bells
and parallel bars, over and over,
all eyes,

not knowing where to look
or when to leave, till he suddenly
shakes his body free, showers at full blast
under the corner tap,

and gently booms, 'I've to go home, boys',
like every day, and leaves, never
to come back, but to become
a sulphurous foreman

in a matchstick factory, well-known
for the fury of his yellow moustache,
once Jatti, wrestler, our teacher
at the gym.

He too Was a Light Sleeper Once

He too was a light sleeper once.

A chuckle in the hall,
the pulse in the neck of a bird
that felt like his own,
a bloodred beak in a lime
tree, a nightmare prince,
anything at all
could wake him to coffee and a mountain-climb
of words on a page.

But now, after sudden jail
and long exile,
fruitbats in his family tree,
marriage of his heart's
little bird
to a clawing cat,
cigarette burns
on children's most private parts,
and the daily caw
at the window
of quarrelling carrion birds,

he just turns,
champs a curse in his jaw
as he gathers his heap
of limbs to climb again to other slopes of sleep,

the iron taste of print in his mouth.

Highway Stripper

Once as I was travelling
on a highway
to Mexico
behind a battered once-blue
Mustang
with a dusty rear window,
the wind really sang
for me

when suddenly
out of the side
of the speeding car
in front of me
a woman's hand
with a wrist-watch on it
threw away
a series of whirling objects
on to the hurtling road:

a straw
hat,
a white shoe fit
to be a fetish,
then another,
a heavy pleated skirt
and a fluttery
slip, faded pink,
frayed lace-edge
and all
(I even heard it swish),
a leg-of-mutton blouse
just as fluttery.

And as I stepped
on the gas
and my car lunged
into the fifty feet
between me
and them,
a rather ordinary,
used, and off-white bra
for smallish
breasts whirled off
the window
and struck
a farmer's barbed wire
with yellow-green wheat grass
beyond
and spread-eagled on it,
pinned
by the blowing wind.

Then before I knew,
bright red panties
laced with white
hit
my windshield
and I flinched,
I swerved,
but then
it was gone,
swept aside
before I straightened up—
fortunately, no one else
on the road:

excited, curious
to see the stripper
on the highway,
maybe with an urgent
lover's one free hand
(or were there more?)
on her breast
or thigh,
I stepped again
on the gas, frustrated by their
dusty rear window
at fifty feet,
I passed them
at seventy.

In that absolute
second,
that glimpse and after-
image in this hell
of voyeurs, I saw
only one at the wheel:
a man,
about forty,

a spectacled profile
looking only
at the road
beyond the nose
of his Mustang,
with a football
radio on.

Again and again
I looked
in my rearview
mirror
as I steadied my pace

against the circling trees,
but there was only
a man:

had he stripped
not only hat
and blouse, shoes
and panties
and bra,
had he shed maybe
even the woman
he was wearing,

or was it me
moulting, shedding
vestiges,
old investments,
rushing forever
towards a perfect
coupling
with naked nothing
in a world
without places?

Middle Age

1

Vietnam eyes my children in the sandbox
  as she splatters my neighbour's tall blond son,
while Biafra gives me

potbellied babies with copper-red
  hungry hair, pellagra scales,
and perpetual pink eyes.

I hold them close from famine to famine
  looking for mothers and penguin nuns,
fighting off

their little mouths from my dry
  fatherly nipples.

2

Half a heart working, the other half
  waiting for an attack from behind
the railing,

all my computers housed in one left lobe,
  the leftover right a temple flagstone
with the temple gone,

keeping safe a nest of purple
  immortal worms from the local
one-eyed raucous crows

and imported Mexican toucans.

3

Reason, locked out of the chicken coop,
    fearful of eagles it cannot see,
pecks at causes,

looks for reasons, grain among pebbles;
    even my belief in unbelief,
that henpecked coxcomb,

crows piteously aloud for a crumb of faith,
    and I look around to see nobody
is watching,

even I, wedded to doubt
    and only married to a woman,
yield, resist,

but inch towards the gypsy tents
    of witchcraft, casting horoscopes
at nightfall,

and manage to think the zodiac
    circulates my blood, that I'm Pisces,
fish out of water,

and my love a motherly Cancer.

Extended Family

Yet like grandfather
I bathe before the village crow

the dry chlorine water
my only Ganges

the naked Chicago bulb
a cousin of the Vedic sun

slap soap on my back
like father

and think
in proverbs

like me
I wipe myself dry

with an unwashed
Sears turkish towel

like mother
I hear faint morning song

(though here it sounds
Japanese)

and three clear strings
nextdoor

through kitchen
clatter

like my little daughter
I play shy

hand over crotch
my body not yet full

of thoughts novels
and children

I hold my peepee
like my little son

play garden hose
in and out
the bathtub

like my grandson
I look up

unborn
at myself

like my great
great-grandson

I am not yet
may never be

my future
dependent

on several
people

yet
to come

The Difference

The women mould a core of clay and straw,
wind around it
strings of beeswax on which the men

do the fine work of eyes and toenails,
picking
with hot needles the look in the eyes;

cover it with a second shell of clay
and pour eight
metals through a hole in the head,

the same escape hole, some would say,
that opens
for the Hindu soul at death.

When they bake the pot of the inchoate god
it makes faces,
exchanging metal for wax, an eye

for an eye, changing its state
as it cools,
when they take a knife to it and hack it

in two to discover the gleaming god.
They leave in
the core of clay for the heavier gods,

or else they'll fall on their faces.

It's with leftovers they make horses, toys;
life scenes of women
pounding rice with lifted pestles;

171

boys; or a drummer girl playing
with both hands
the two-headed drum for two dancers

with long brazen necks, long legs, long hands,
arrested in a whirl.

ii

But I, a community of one,
mould
myself both clay and metal,

body shape and lips; do my dancers first,
jet bombers
and tiny Taj Mahals for tourists

these days, then come through pestles,
women,
and horses to the gods who will bake

only if time permits, if there's metal left,
and desire,
or if my children's quarrels need new gods

for playthings. But today, out of the blue,
when Vishnu
came to mind, the Dark One you know

who began as a dwarf and rose in the world
to measure
heaven and earth with his paces,

I found I'd just enough left to fashion
his big toe,
and as I stare at this left toe and toenail

172

weighing on my hand, I can tell perhaps
the height
of this image as elephant trainers can

the height and gender of a runaway
elephant
by the size of his footprint in wet grass,

but I know I've no way at all of telling
the look,
if any, on his face, or of catching

the rumoured beat of his extraordinary heart.

Dancers in a Hospital

1

Spinoza grinding lenses brings me
    into focus, and I see my small brown
hand as a species

of eternity, when I go head first
    through a blueblack windshield in a red car,
fleeing news of riot

in the black white city, waking
    not quite awake, not quite dead, coming out
garbled, with a thick tongue,

rinsing out with chemicals
    a catarrh of consonants, the vowels
a whistle in the nose;

the head a gauze cocoon of bandages,
    a chrysalis among thorn trees and nurses,
I think of flight

while my leg, a separate mummy
    in a hospital stirrup, dreams as if
under pentothal

of Naga dancers.

2

Underground trains jogging through my sleep,
    my time's hurrying chariots, always
behind me in my walks

to the grocery in Bombay or Moscow,
    a rattle of shaking jowls, midnight heads
in crumpled hats, wet

newspapers with a seepage of backpage
    news in international latrines,
with Reagan or Mao

under our feet.

Moulting

Moulting has first to find a thorn at a suitable height to pin and fix the growing numbness in the tail. Then it can begin to slough and move out of that loose end, whole though flayed alive.

That's how you see now and then a dry skin or two hanging, and you may be sickened for a minute by a thin old snake vacillating and pale on a black thorn, working out a new body on a fence you just defiled.

Lord of snakes and eagles, and everything in between, cover my son with an hour's shade and be the thorn at a suitable height in his hour of change.

Some People

Others see a rush, a carnival, a million,
why does he see nothing, or worse, just one:

a singular body, a familiar head?
You'd worry too, wouldn't you, if,

in a whole milling conference
on Delhi milk and China soybean, in all

that human hair, national
smells and international fragrance,

you saw your wife from another life,
wed and left behind in childhood,

now six weeks dead, yet standing there
in raw-silk sari, in sandalwood footwear?

Connect!

Connect! Connect! cries my disconnecting
    madness, remembering phrases.
See the cycles,

father whispers in my ear, black holes
    and white noise, elections with four-year
shadows, red eclipses

and the statistics of rape. Connect,
    connect, beasts with monks, slave economies
and the golden bough.

But my watchers are silent as if
    they knew my truth is in fragments.
If they could, I guess

they would say, only the first thought
    is clear, the second is dim,
the third is ignorant

and it takes a lot of character
    not to call it mystery, to endure
the fog, and search

the mango grove unfolding leaf and twig
    for the zebra-striped caterpillar
in the middle of it,

waiting for a change of season.

Looking and Finding

Looking for a system, he finds a wife. Was it Vallejo who said,
'How anger breaks down a man into children!'?

Searching for mankind, he travels third class, a carrier for
flu, bedbugs, eczema, and anarchist ideas: loses friends who fear
all symptoms, any contact with any contact with possible syphilis.

Dreams are full of enemies, bruises; his wife scrubs his chest
with rough compassion and lysol. That evening he beats up his
three-year old son for laughing at him.

A stillness haunts his walking, there's a fury in his sitting
quiet. He can neither sleep nor wake from the one-legged sleep
on this Chicago lake of yachts in full sail, herons playing at sages.

Having no clear conscience, he looks for one in the morning
news. Assam then, Punjab now, finds him guilty of an early
breakfast of two whole poached eggs.

Attacked and defended by dying armies, the wounds find no
blood on him, his bathroom cupboard is full of unused band-
aids.

Thirsty, he finds the red of the wine slimy with the blood of
bees, the wetness of water mossy with the fibre of the disinfected
worm.

Calves' teeth in the foaming milk rattle in his mouth. The
sugarcane worker's sickle wheels in the candy, cuts the palate,
slits the tongue.

O alewives floating on my poison lake, he cries at 3 a.m., I
wish I could feed myself to your fellow fish on my dinnerplate.

179

Love Poem for a Wife and Her Trees

i

Dear woman, you never let me forget
what I never quite remember:
you're not Mother,

certified dead but living on, close
to her children, tinkling in glass-
bead curtains,

peacock patterns shivering in three cities.
You remind me of the difference
especially

on panic's zenith, on the unattended
Ferris wheel rickety in the wind,
lest I collapse

into a son, destroy the intricate
diagrams of Dravidian kinship
where triangles

marry only circles descended
from other triangles and circles
in the notebooks

of anthropologists sitting
on family trees, those topsy-
turvy trees

with their roots in heaven
and branches in the earth.

180

Dear woman, you remind me again
in unlikely places like post offices
where I lick

your stamps, that I must remember
you're not my Daughter, unborn maybe
but always

present: lest I, like your nightmare
father-king, try to save you from the world,
that Grisly Beard,

that phantom son-in-law, save you even
from your own heart's madness, save you
from all things

messy and fertile, from all images
but mine; lock you deep in my male
and royal coffers,

impregnable wombs of metal, and throw away
the key in the alligator moat.
Out of touch,

deprived of traffic, now an ant-world
down below, seen from a fortieth floor,
nose pressed to window,

in the safe custody of an anti-
septic bubble, your spinal cord
will wither—

that stem of all senses, that second tree
with the root at the top, branches branching
in limb and lung,

down to toe, hangnail, and fingertip.

I forget at night and remember at dawn
you're not me but Another, the faraway
stranger who's nearby,

like the Blue Mountain tree in the cuttings
of my garden graft, or its original,
sighted once

up close in my telescope, seasoned and alive
with leaf, bud, monkeys, birds, pendant
bats, parasites,

patch of blue scilla lilies in its shade;
exotic who inhabits my space
but migrates

to Panamas of another
childhood; one half of me, often
occupying all,

yet ever ready to call a taxi
and go away; foreign body
with a mind

that knows what I'll never know:
languages of the deep south, weathers,
underground faults

in my own continent, mushrooms
for love and hate, backrubs and sinister
witchery, how

to buy the perfect pomfret for dinner
in a world of stranded fish,
or pluck the one

red apple in the garden for dessert
from the one tree that's not upside down,
its mother root

unfolding in the earth a mirror image
of every branch and twig thrust deep
into the sky.

iv

Yet I know you'll play at Jewish mama,
sob-sister, daughter who needs help
with arithmetic,

even the sexpot nextdoor, topless
tree spirit on a temple frieze,
or plain Indian wife

at the village well, so I can play son,
father, brother, macho lover, gaping
tourist, and clumsy husband.

Looking for the Centre

1

Looking for the centre these days
   is like looking for the Center
for Missing Children

which used to be here, but now has moved
   downtown to a new building, southwest
of the Loop,

kitty corner from the Second Chicago
   Movers, last room to the left on the fifth
floor. Ask there

for the Center, anyone will tell you.

2

Looking for the centre is a job
   for eccentrics who can feel the thirteen
motions of the earth

when they stand still in the middle
   of the market: you too feel the galaxies
moving, as they talk

about pebbles. That evening you open
   an old anatomy textbook where
pictures in flesh tones

unfold a human body, layer
   under layer, skin, muscle, ganglia
of nerves, branching red

or blue veins, stomach, liver, pancreas
   and spleen, but then you open that last flap,
under the crimson

184

pair of kidneys, you plunge headlong—
    dandruff, doubts, and all—into a map
of the heavens.

3

Intoxicated by the body's toxins,
    liquors brewed in gland and gonad,
a zilla spider

on LSD, I spin enormous webs
    in a Tahiti forest of April twigs,
unaware

in my ecstasy I'm not at the centre,
    do not feel the tug of spidersilk,
for the web

has gaps any moth can fall through
    to safety, and live on to make more moths,
to make more holes

in royal brocades, my routine
    symmetries blown by the carelessness
of simple chemistry.

4

Suddenly, connections severed
    as in a lobotomy, unburdened
of history, I lose

my bearings, a circus zilla spun
    at the end of her rope, dizzy,
terrified,

and happy. And my watchers
    watch, cool as fires
in a mirror.

185

Chicago Zen

i

Now tidy your house,
dust especially your living room

and do not forget to name
all your children.

ii

Watch your step. Sight may strike you
blind in unexpected places.

The traffic light turns orange
on 57th and Dorchester, and you stumble,

you fall into a vision of forest fires,
enter a frothing Himalayan river,

rapid, silent.

On the 14th floor,
Lake Michigan crawls and crawls

in the window. Your thumbnail
cracks a lobster louse on the windowpane

from your daughter's hair
and you drown, eyes open,

towards the Indies, the antipodes.
And you, always so perfectly sane.

Now you know what you always knew:
the country cannot be reached

by jet. Nor by boat on jungle river,
hashish behind the Monkey-temple,

nor moonshot to the cratered Sea
of Tranquillity, slim circus girls

on a tightrope between tree and tree
with white parasols, or the one

and only blue guitar.

                    Nor by any
other means of transport,

migrating with a clean valid passport,
no, not even by transmigrating

without any passport at all,
but only by answering ordinary

black telephones, questions
walls and small children ask,

and answering all calls of nature.

                    iv
Watch your step, watch it, I say,
especially at the first high
threshold,

           and the sudden low
one near the end
of the flight
of stairs,

        and watch
for the last
step that's never there.

188

Waterfalls in a Bank

And then one sometimes sees waterfalls
   as the ancient Tamils saw them,
wavering snakeskins,

cascades of muslin. Sometimes
   in the spray, living and dying children
tumble towards old age,

lovesongs, and Biafra, orchestras in bombsites,
   hunger's saints in the glasshouse alley,
and more children,

with a bentover grandmother, black
   and wrinkled as a raisin, working
between mother's labouring

thighs, in a corner room with steaming
   gleaming brass vats, and four lemons
for good omens.

As I transact with the past as with another
   country with its own customs, currency,
stock exchange, always

at a loss when I count my change: water-
   falls of dying children, Assam
politics,

and downtown Nairobi fall through me
   in Hyde Park Bank, as I rise among them,
mud on my nose,

a rhododendron rising from a compost
   of rhododendrons, chicken bones,
silk of girlish hair,

and the nitrogen of earthworms.

As I hear the waters fall, the papers
    rustle, and it's evening: a paralytic sadhu,
tapdancer of the St. Vitus's dance,

knocking his steps out on the pebbles
    with no reflexes left in either knee,
lifts with his one good finger

his loincloth, and pisses standing
    like a horse on my childhood's dark
sidestreet, aiming his stream

at two red flowers on the oleander bush,
    as a car turns the corner.
Headlights make his arc

a trajectory of yellow diamonds,
    scared instant rainbows, ejecting spurts
of crystal, shocked

by the commonplace cruelty of headlights.

January here: a seven-day snowfall
    covers Chicago, clogs the traffic,
grounds the planes;

muffles screams, garbage cans, pianos;
    topples a mayor and elects another
who promises clearance

of debts and snowfalls with their silent
    white effects, tickertape on astronauts,
white flower on black thorn.

And my watchers watch, from their nowhere perches.

Second Sight

In Pascal's endless queue,
people pray, whistle, or make

remarks. As we enter the dark,
someone says from behind,

'You are Hindoo, aren't you?
You must have second sight.'

I fumble in my nine
pockets like the night-blind

son-in-law groping
in every room for his wife,

and strike a light to regain
at once my first, and only,

sight.

Book Four

The Black Hen (1995)

The Black Hen

It must come as leaves
to a tree
or not at all

yet it comes sometimes
as the black hen
with the red round eye

on the embroidery
stitch by stitch
dropped and found again

and when it's all there
the black hen stares
with its round red eye

and you're afraid

Foundlings in the Yukon

In the Yukon the other day
miners found the skeleton
of a lemming
curled around some seeds
in a burrow:
sealed off by a landslide
in Pleistocene times.

Six grains were whole,
unbroken: picked and planted
ten thousand
years after their time,
they took root
within forty-eight hours
and sprouted
a candelabra of eight small leaves.

A modern Alaskan lupine,
I'm told, waits three years to come
to flower, but these
upstarts drank up sun
and unfurled early
with the crocuses of March
as if long deep
burial had made them hasty

for birth and season, for names,
genes, for passing on:
like the kick
and shift of an intra-uterine
memory, like
this morning's dream of being
born in an eagle's
nest with speckled eggs and the screech

of nestlings, like a pent-up
centenarian's sudden burst
of lust, or maybe
just elegies in Duino unbound
from the dark,
these new aborigines biding
their time
for the miner's night-light

to bring them their dawn,
these infants compact with age,
older than the oldest
things alive, having skipped
a million falls
and the registry of tree-rings,
suddenly younger
by an accident of flowering

than all their timely descendants.

Dream in an Old Language

Sunlit tree frog at the lake
doesn't know

the shade is the enemy's shadow.

Moves from egg to tadpole
to adult, to grow

from water to land and back:

then every night he struggles
in the mouth of a snake

too old to swallow, too hungry to let go

of his prey till at light of day
the frog hops

away from his nightly enemy

adding one more fear now
to cat and crow,

a terror of creepers and ropes.

Shadows

Shadows fall between people
when they walk in the sun.
Doubts grow in the dark
and by dawn the window
is tangled in vines.

Scaffoldings grid the steeple
when time's work is done.
Moss grows on the bark
of the oak, wrinkles on a brow,
as men explode stepping on mines.

Women circumambulate the peepul
tree hoping for a son.
Daughters breed in stark
family dungeons like slow
perennials waiting for the rains.

War heroes return in special trains
covered with blood and flags. They blow
bugles at home, brawl in pubs, and bark
orders at dogs, kill and flay twenty-one
nurses and hang one from a maple.

2 January 1992

At Zero,

clocks lose their tongues,
        the hands fall off,
spider legs: pendulums sway
        no more, scrotums
of dead bulls: timepieces
        on wrists and towers

lose time,

blank brahmin-widow faces,
        though the wheels turn, the cogs
catch: at the centre of the white,
        black, or coin face,
the axle, dot of metal, turns
        continually: the twelve

numbers

say nothing, untouched
        by any hand: time circles
making no mark in space:
        space, once crammed
with places and things, red-
        bricks in the mauve

distance,

wavers with the trees
        in the heat haze behind
a plane waiting
        for take-off: the eye looks,
cannot see anything
        but currents of vapor

curling

in the transparency:
        the ear listens, cannot hear
a thing: only the finger-
        tip senses the movement
of a balance wheel somewhere
        in there like a dove

pulsing:

now faint, now clear,
        in a blind man's hand:
at zero, as when the potter-saint
        singing hymns, dancing
his god, kneaded with his feet
        the soft red clay, burying

alive his youngest child.

Salamanders

Again, here it comes, the nothing,
the zero where numbers die or begin,
the sunless day, the moonless month,
where sounds do not become words
nor words the rivals of silence.

How describe this nothing
we, of all things, flee in panic
yet wish for, work towards,
build ships and shape whole cities with?

Salamanders I'd heard live
in fire and drink the flame
as we the air: but when I met
them in the sludge of September

woods after rain, they were ember-
red but cold, born new and blind,
naked earthlings, poor yet satin
to the eye, velvet to the touch.

We, denizens of this nowhere nothing,
flame within black flame, where red
marries green and annuls it in the act,
yellow shade in yellow shadow, empty hub
of the turning wheel, mother and father

of the forever unborn, obeying edicts
written in smoke by war for countries
that never were—we, we burn
and eat fire no less than salamanders

but live in the wet, crawl in the slush,
five-toed lizards eating dragonflies,
waiting no less than the three-toed for a turn
of the body's season to copulate and people
the woods with babies satin to the eye

and velvet to the touch, surprising
only Hollywood Aliens who know us only
through legends or medieval woodcuts,
who suddenly meet us one day, blind,
actual, underfoot in the woods.

Traces

The stars are constellations
only to an eye light years away.
They do not even belong
to the same time or galaxy
except on the earth
that reads its fate in the Seven
Sages and the Milky Way.

Oceans swirl around earthlings
giving them shores, beaches, marinas,
vacations, continents, harbors,
ships and submarines, undersea
kingdoms, whalesong, moontides,
The Tempest, Moby Dick,
and Robinson Crusoe.

The earth itself has layers of time,
shelves of fossils that carry traces
of anything that will leave a trace,
like seed, shell, a leaf pressed
on clay, wingbone and cowskull,
waiting for people to decipher
and give themselves a past
and a family tree.

22 March 1993

Fire

Brown eyes, family faces, maculate giraffes
jiggle and disappear. Blue streaks flash
through floating smoke, indigo
nudes streaking through a seacoast
lit sidelong by a red sun-disk
here, in this living room.

Ordinary wood blocks delivered at the door.
A box of matches bought at the corner store.
And here this supernatural fire that can burn
the house down, maybe the whole neighborhood,
Simla and California, the hill a long horse
with orange hair.

15 March 1992

Birthdays

Birthdays come and go,
for brother, son, daughter,
spouse, niece and nephew,
and among them, mine, and as I grow
older, they come as often as death
anniversaries in all the families
I know,
and they linger under tamarind
trees like other absences.

Even universities,
art museums, apple trees
that recycle the seasons,
and inventions like guns
have their birthdays
like St Francis, Shakespeare,
Gandhi and Washington
marked on calendars.

Birth takes a long time
though death can be sudden,
and multiple, like pregnant deer
shot down on the run.
Yet one would like to think,
one kicks and grabs the air
in death throes as a baby
does in its mother's womb
months before the event.

There's no evidence as far
as I can see, which isn't
very far, to say that death
throes are birth pangs.
Birth seems quite special
every time a mayfly is born
into the many miracles
of day, night and twilight,

but death? Is it a dispersal
of gathered energies
back into their elements,
earth, air, water, and fire,
a reworking into other moulds,
grass, worm, bacterial glow
lights, and mother-matter
for other off-spring with names
and forms clocked into seasons?

16 March 1992

Fog

Stuck in the need to move on,
eyes turn round and round,
oxen at the oil-press.

Waiting for change, the body
changes, a chrysalis
that will rot unless it breaks

into wings. Restless, unable to move,
claustrophobic in elevators,
those prisons that move on their own,

hands strain against the present tense,
a labyrinth with cement pillars,
trees without leaf or season,

legs running without moving, finding
nowhere everywhere, a swirl
of fog that lifts an hour at a time,

a cold that burns without blisters,
pulse ticking off time like
an umpire over a fallen wrestler.

18 March 1992

One More on a Deathless Theme

This body I sometimes call me,
sometimes mine,
as if I'm someone else
owning and informing this body
that affects me most when it affects
another by look,

touch, odour and pulse, its blue
and red revolutions
of blood and even out-of-body
ecstasies, making possible
whenever it can with another
body,

a momentary legend, a mythic
beast with two backs,
mammal and quadruped, even
a four-armed androgyne like our god
who used to be everywhere but is now housed
in the kitchen,

will one day be short of breath,
lose its thrust,
turn cold, dehydrate and leave
a jawbone with half a grin
near a pond: just as this dog
I walk

to let him pass water and express
his waste
so he may frisk and slobber happily
all day, or moan at the gate
for that female in the street,
will turn cold

like her and her nuzzling suitors
who cannot rest
till they give her puppies
and grand-puppies,
will be buried with an apple tree
planted on her to burst
into blossom in April,

to be eaten as a red-green apple
in a windfall.
Everyone in this street
will become cold, lie under stones
or be scattered as ash
in rivers and oceans.

2

Thinking of ash, I fall
asleep.
'I'm your older twin, senior
by five minutes,' says an orange
Persian cat, as he climbs on my lap
and begins to give

advice on how to play checkers
in last night's
dream and, though I've forgotten
what he said, his purr stays
with me till noon as I go about
in downtown buses

looking without looking for an orange
Persian cat
as if nothing at all is happening,
as if the dog, his female, me
and my warm-blooded mate who makes me
for a long lightning

moment a God Whose One Half
is Woman,
and all these people in this street
and all the other streets everywhere,
even the bluebottles on the dog-do
begetting bluebottles

on bluebottles, those sapphires
among flies,
and the praying mantis astride
on another praying mantis,
green and still on the seasoned
apple tree,

would be forever there
waiting for me
as they've always done
for astronauts anytime they return
from faraway Jupiters
or just downtown.

August

August was hot
and so was September.
Three of my brothers
and my two sisters
were all born in August
and September.

November was cold
and December was icy.
Mother died in November
and Father had a stroke
in December.

January, looking forward
and backward like the gatekeeper
god, was hot inside
and winter out: first love
and lovers' quarrels.

The next three months
were tepid like the coffee
in grandmother's village house.
Hibernations for bears
and a cat-mouse marriage.

April to June burned
night and day like
a temple lamp kept alive
by a cripple praying
for her legs

and July was at war,
bombs overhead,
napalm fires in the bone,
children almost drowned
in a flash flood

of divorce papers.

7 September 1991

Three Dreams

In the first,
this man had twenty-one
daughters.

Then I received a fellowship
for me, my wife, son and daughter,
and my dog, to do research
on happiness for three hours
on Monday, the 17th of March.

Before I knew it
I was in a ruined house
lit by rays of dust in the light
seeping through the cracks
and the broken windows.
I had a microphone
to report
on the ruins.

It

I see it out there like a small
tree with two broken branches
between two gnarled oaks lifting
their full head of leaves
into the rain,

but I don't know how to get down
from this guest room window
on the third floor attic
down the turning stair into Judy's
computer room,
not be waylaid by the toilet
where the calico cat laps water
from the white well,
and down the stairs on to the Baluchi
dyed-in-blood rug, out on
the verandah, step down two more wood-block steps
to the gravel textured against the wet
grass straight as cropped Chinese hair,

to the small tree with two broken branches
out there, below my mind,
in the back of my tongue. I hear it
running like an underground Ganges
under my feet, over my head,
like leaky taps upstairs and downstairs,
purring at my side like the kitchen fridge,
inside me like tummy gurgles,

always running from me,
water tables under a Tantalus
forever thirsty, forever surrounded
by the sounds and white flashes
of rapids that drench, pull, tickle and unbalance
his feet but cannot wet his throat.

Not Knowing

1

not knowing what to say to her
I walk into the park
and watch the sparrows

she is sitting on a green bench
watching sparrows

2

not knowing how to beat him up
in my rage I strike the walls
and hit my head

till blood streams down my cheeks
he takes me home and bandages my head

3

not knowing who I am or what I want
I roam the city walk into movies
hurtle down a roller coaster

till mirrors in a mirror shop
break me up into how many I was
show me in profile and fragment

whose head I have whose nose
how tall how old my hair
how black my shoes how red

like clocks in the clockshop
quartz digital grandfather and mickey
mouse each showing a different

time all at once

On Not Learning from Animals

Animals bring us tranquillity. Cats
sleep through a war. Dogs ignore your sister's
cancer, forgive betrayals and rations,
while all morning a man cannot bear his own
betrayal after sleeping with two women.
But a dog will not mount one bitch after
another nor want to kill himself
for being a cad:

              and quails are monogamous,
says the encyclopaedia. The baboon
has a harem but he is not tormented
by claims for equal time. But then
I forget how troubled I was when I saw,
at seventeen, after quarrelling
with my father about my mother's rights,
a female ape with a black striped snout
sort out patiently with her long hands, then
sniff, and lick lettuce leaves clean for her lord
and master while he growled all through.

4 January 1992

Blind Spots

Eyes cannot follow
a bird
over the hill.

Ears hear a whistle,
a wheel,
but not the grass.

Hands reach, even catch
the curve
of a curly hair

but not a thought
in the air
read between lovers.

Noses know when any-
thing burns
anywhere but cannot

learn the smell of fear.

LOVE 1: *what she said*

His eyes are moss-green.
His blood is cold.
His heart is a piece
of lead.

His face is razor-lean.
His liver is on hold.
He raped his niece.
She's dead.
His mother's mean.
They've stabbed and sold
puppies and monkeys
for bread.

    Yet I grow lean.
    His heart is gold
    to my greed. My eyes
    are fed

    when he turns his head.

11 January 1990

Sonnet

Time moves in and out of me
a stream of sound, a breeze,
an electric current that seeks
the ground, liquids that transpire

through my veins, stems and leaves
toward the skies to make fog and mist
around the trees. Mornings brown
into evenings before I turn around

in the day. Postage stamps, words
of unwritten letters complete with commas,
misplaced leases and passports, excuses
and blame swirl through the night

and take me far away from home
as time moves in and out of me.

8 January 1992

220

Mythologies 1

The breast she offered was full
of poison and milk.
Flashing eyes suddenly dull,
her voice was silk.

The Child took her breast
in his mouth and sucked it right out of her chest.
Her carcass stretched from north to south.

She changed, undone by grace,
from deadly mother to happy demon,
found life in death.

O Terror with a baby face,
suck me dry. Drink my venom.
Renew my breath.

LOVE 2: *what he said, groping*

Taking off glasses
estranges places,
reduces literacy
to the largest print.
Lights loom, dead
oranges in a fog.
Faces move
under water.
You no longer see
eye to eye.

A hand wrapped in a glove
can no longer pick
a dime off the floor,
or a carrot-red
hair. Or thread
a needle. Or feel the fuzz
on a peach
or a familiar cheek.
You see, smell, hear
what you cannot touch.

That drug
for the racing pulse
puts sleep
into waking,
moves the sidewalk
far away and slow
under someone else's
feet. All day it's late
afternoon and 3:20
always in the radium dark.

Loving someone
not in love
is to lose one's glasses
underfoot without a language
in a village
fair, to wake up without fingers,
to drug the heart
and slow down a world.

1990

Turning Around

turning around I see a flock of sheep
in a tree-filtered slant of sunlight
gilding a cloud of dust

coming towards me, black, white,
walking clouds of wool
with downcast faces

behind them a man in a dirty
red turban and a brown
rough blanket

wielding a stick and a shepherd's
throaty cry probably learned from
his father now blind

and sitting in the sun
outside his hut smoking
bidis all day

but what am I to this herd
of Indian sheep, to be fed
and sheared or

slaughtered, or to this man
who shares a throaty cry
with his father

and his father's father,
his cousins and enemies
for miles around?

11 December 1991

LOVE 3: *what he said, remembering*

The hours brown,
bloodtide more ebb
than flow,
the flaming bush
now ash,
I wake as if
sleep was work.

Mother's crown
a patch of scab,
her eye now slow,
'No rush',
she says as I wash
her face in fear
I'd run berserk

as years fall, downtown
in the rain-soaked cab,
my baby sister asleep
in her lap,
she offers me her breast:
'No rush', she says
as I fall to work

and suckle till I glow
on milk still warm, groan
at the taste
of Mother's salt,
and Oedipus,
five, weaned, and jealous,
seems no longer halt
or blind: cured almost.

3 February 1990

Mythologies 2

When the clever man asks the perfect boon:
not to be slain by demon, god, or by
beast, not by day nor by night,
by no manufactured weapon, not out
of doors nor inside, not in the sky
nor on earth,

             come now come soon,
Vishnu, man, lion, neither and both, to hold
him in your lap to disembowel his pride
with the steel glint of bare claws at twilight.

O midnight sun, eclipse at noon,
net of loopholes, a house all threshold,
connoisseur of negatives and assassin
of certitudes, slay now my faith in doubt.
End my commerce with bat and night-
owl. Adjust my single eye, rainbow bubble,
so I too may see all things double.

July 1992

LOVE 4: *what he said, to his daughter*

I love him, she said
at eighteen.
But he's seventy,

I said, forgetting
at sixty three
that all the women

I've ever loved
have stayed eighteen
forever.

Pierre Bonnard
always painted his wife
as thirty six

getting in and out
of bathtubs, sleek,
naked on diamond

squares of blue tile
till she was seventy
three.

31 March 1992

Mythologies 3

'Keep off when I worship Siva.
Touch me three times, and you'll never
see me again', said Akka to her new groom
who couldn't believe his ears:

                                   Om, Om!
she seemed to intone in bed with every breath
and all he could think of was her round breast,
her musk, her darling navel and the rest.
So he hovered and touched her, her body death-

ly cold to mortal touch but hot for God's
first move, a caress like nothing on earth.
She fled his hand as she would a spider,

threw away her modesty, as the rods
and cones of her eyes gave the world a new birth:
She saw Him then, unborn, form of forms, the Rider,

His white Bull chewing cud in her backyard.

LOVE 5

Though, at night, or anytime at all
in bed, he flashes lightnings, strips stark
naked, won't even wait for the half-dark
to watch her watch him rise and fall,

wants the lights on when she takes off
her underthings, to see her resume
her natural curves and catch the waft
of odours transcending all perfume,

to kiss her deep, say unspeakable things
to her back and front in whisper and joke,
taste her juices at their sources, stoke
the smithy all hours to hammer rings

of gold out of touch and taste—he's stunned by
daylight, he stammers and his looks are shy.

8 – 22 February 1993

Contraries

Blinking in the light
she stares into midnight.
Crowded by the dark
her eyes see glowing monarch
butterflies.

Flying through the air
he feels earthworms in his hair.
As he burrows through the ground,
herons fly round and round
in his eyes.

Dying of hunger with African
children, he feels like a fat pelican
eating peanuts in a winter garden.
Beauty is now ugly, sad is glad,
truths are lies

when, living by contraries,
his roots are topsyturvy trees,
rivers mirrors of heat,
long-dead faces fish at his feet,
and ears have eyes.

Engagement

I shouldn't have been surprised
that engagement meant
so many things:

betrothal, the moment
of the ring and the double
heartbeat of panic;

battle, aerial dogfight,
the smoke of war
on faces;

the twist in the gut
of an indifferent house-
holder's conversion

to a cause; and that 'point
when the baby stops floating
around and its head

wedges down into the mother's
pelvis in the delivery
position'.

The Day Went Dark

I bought a carpet
with orange flowers
and green leaves

but all my furniture
looked bilious yellow
in its gorgeous light.

I loved a woman
with turquoise eyes,
navel like a whirlpool

in a heap of wheat

and the day went dark
my hands were lizards,
my heart turned into a hound.

19 December 1991

LOVE 6: *winter*

Green leaves on a grey tree
look almost like flowers,
sudden smiles on a chickenpox
face, or an accidental
touch between quarrels.

Though blindness cannot see,
it can hear the hours
chime, now close now far, from clocks
across my shop-window city, a hall
of mirrors for squirrels,

till the blind eye begins
to look for grey within grey,
skyscrapers in silhouette,
every cell lit in gold
without waiting for night:

but unseeing, the eye within
wants only red or green on grey,
to sense in winter the heat,
translate new signals in old
ways, taking the dark for light.

25 February 1993

That Tree

The legendary tree is upside down.
Roots in the air, branches in the ground.

Dig under your eyes, enter a world
where earth is sky, branches curled

under branches. Another earth firm
below it, aptly wet, dry, cold, or warm,

three quarters sea with a coral reef
in its Australian corner, where killer

fish grow up to smile on smaller
fry, where warmth and beauty are food,

a worm's life an allegory of the good.
Stop there! Burn that tree of wishful hashish.

See the leprosy next door in the gold leaf
of that fire. Cover your body with the ash

of that underground heaven, that topsy-turvy
crescent, for no myth can cure leprosy.

PAIN: *trying to find a metaphor*

I never knew I could bear pain.
But then I never knew about acid

rain. A nerve in the vice of a cyst
in the bone, a growth like a bonsai tree

spreading like smoke in the mist of an X-ray,
vague as a face in a corridor on fire,

remembers a rogue elephant managed by three
tame ones that once were rogues,

rattles my chains, back to childhood
bellows silent screams while flaming tongues

flick at my bone, a house on invisible fire
with a household of all my selves turning

slowly to black skeletons in the orange
glow, and then to charred flesh and ash,

swirling around one absurdly alive and well,
walking familiar streets, talking to himself

as always with gesture, grimace, and head-shakes
as if to an idiot child full of linguistic questions.

8 December 1992

Fizzle

His blood, Stravinsky used to say,
was thick, getting thicker.
He was afraid he would crystallize
into rubies if he didn't keep drinking
beer and whiskey.

T.S. Eliot said, his German doctor
found his blood the thinnest
he had ever seen and prescribed
thick soups, oat meal and spinach
pasta every day.

Osteoporosis, my neighbor says,
makes bones brittle. Her doctors
are afraid she would one day
hear her skeleton crack beginning
with the backbone.

Watch it crumble. Watch the soul
watch both itself and its corporeal
twin sweat, dry out, ache, burn,
flicker, the seer and the seen
fizzle towards nothing.

236

A Devotee's Complaint

Try to curry favor
with Lakshmi,
you lose an eye-tooth.

Saraswati, she slaps you hard
and where her fingers touch
your cheek, you've no hair

so you've to shave close
or bear her four-finger mark
on your face.

If Siva touches you—
when you cut your finger
in the kitchen

not blood but ash spills
from your cut as it did
for that ascetic

who dried out for Siva.

In March

In March I travelled
not by train or bus or plane
but through the bloodstream
warm as the ocean current
that took Aztecs to Mexico.

Fever showed me alligators
sleeping on the island mounds,
rows of sharp teeth
peeping from irregular mouth-lines
that a small special bird

was allowed to pick
after every meal.
Red-hot fish, the white heat
of whales, blips and signals
of cool silver dolphins

swam all around me
in that gulf stream
circling my continents
through the stillness of icebergs
and sleepless oceans.

I never knew that my Amazon
flows savage and treacherous
through my Africas,
undersea forests and peopled seas
lash nightly on shores

that flicker morning noon
and night as fever cools
healing my third degree
burns with oils mentholated
according to family recipes.

3 March 1992

A Meditation

In the course of a meditation
I thought all day I was a black
walnut tree.

That evening, the golden
retriever from the yellow house
sniffed me

as I stood waiting for the traffic
light, lifted its hind leg
and honoured me

with its warm piss.

In the rainstorm that night, the tree
toppled with a great crash and lay
there, its roots

an exposition in the sky.
The municipality came
with electric

chain-saws, cut it up in convenient
pieces, loaded them in their truck
and took it all

somewhere.

The carpenter worked with his hand saw,
smoothed it with sand paper, polished it
with bees' wax,

made a butcher block table and
a butcher block chair. The paper
factory ground up

the bark and the leaves into a pulp,
patted it, bleached it, and turned out rolls
of paper

with a logo in a watermark.

Now here I sit in this chair,
paper and pencil on my table,
and as I write

I know I'm writing now on my head,
now on my torso, my living
hands moving

on a dead one, a firm imagined body
working with the transience
of breathless

real bodies.

Difficulty

On the difficulty of writing
anything, when little demons
throw colours and hunger

cries tear through the paper
destroy the commas and devour
the passive voice

till lightning in a serial world
of words, strike
the tall bare oak

to cleave it in two
and make it spring
into unlikely leaf

in winter

Poetry and Our City

Working through sonnet forms, he turns
into an alley full of garbage cans
brimming with brown bags and plastic,
some poking through the lid, paws
and hands of creatures struggling to escape.

Trying to learn haikus and tankas, he
burns acacia leaves in the fall,
the smoke acrid with hints
of marijuana, mafia flames, orange
saris torn in strips in a riot.

He settles down to free verse but finds
eyes green as a broken bottle glinting
from a face spattered with cinnamon
freckles, the right half shrivelled and stitched
around half a lip after an accident.

No Fifth Man

after an old Sanskrit parable

Then there is the story
of five brahmans
who go abroad to learn
all the sixty four arts.

When they meet again
in the woods outside
their town, of course
they want to show off.

The first man picks up a bone
at random, not suspecting
it's a tiger's femur,
and blows syllables on it,

surprises himself
by having on his hands
a tiger's skeleton,
when the second man

does his thing: gives it
liver, lungs, arteries
inferior and superior, veins
blue and red fountaining

out of a heart, paws,
claws, a mouthful of fangs, a womb
and a gender though
it's still a sorry thing

looks flayed
though it has never known a skin
makes a tiger a tiger,
fire and velvet,

that pelt of stripes
and gold, which is what
the third brahman give it,
crowing almost with glee.

Now, there!
stood a tiger on all fours
on the forest floor, shawled
with the dotted shade,

about to spring if only
its heart could beat,
its eye could see,
its mouth could water.

Engendered, lifelike but
incapable, as it stood
still, a mere effigy,
it could neither live nor die.

The fourth brahman knew how
to breathe life into it,
was about to do so
when the fifth one,

their boyhood buddy
who had learned nothing,
suddenly said, 'Stop:
Don't. It may eat us all up'.

The fourth one said,
'Of course, I'm giving it life.
I'm its papa. This is
my pussycat. Justy watch'.

The fifth man, the coward,
cried, 'Wait, wait
just one second',
and climbed up a tree in a hurry

244

while the fourth chanted a mantra,
gave the tigress life,
death, a heartbeat,
an eye for prey and

a raging hunger all
at once inspiring
terror in beauty, changing
a nothing into a thing never before,

and the creature pounced on him,
his three friends rooted
in their fear, killed them all
and ate them up for starters.

Nothing was left of them,
not even a bone.

Poetry too is a tigress,
except there's no fifth
man left on a tree
when she takes your breath

away.

22 January 1990

Bulls

Bulls and bulldozers
      block each other
            on the road to Chidambaram.

Ravens caw.
      Fruitbats hang broken
            umbrellas in the branches

of the giant tree.

Ambivalent as a man
      married to two wives
            I walk through the holy place,

one eye wincing, fearing
      beggars and leprosy,
            another on temples, women,

and trees that seem
      to believe in god as if
            he lived and moved between them,

drinking from the gutter,
      suffering eczema, birth pangs, and the slow
            death of the calf in the backyard

and the child in the opposite
      house, flowering red and yellow
            in the gulmohur, laughing in the eyes

of the madman and the bride,
      running as water, burning
            as camphor, mangy as an alley cat,

making language
      like early birds
            or even this page.

Bosnia

How can one write about Bosnia,
Biafra, Bangladesh, just to take
only the atrocities that begin with B,

alphabetize cruelties,
eating persimmons and sleeping safe
in the arms of a lover, a wet moon

in the mullioned window? How file away
the friend just dead of ovarian cancer;
a young breast cigarette-burned by a jealous

husband; where shall I put the old man who peers
through office windows looking for a yes
that'll negate all no's, or Bosnia mothers

who lift their babies to strangers
squabbling for a foothold in lorries fleeing
to the borders where only death waits

gun and milk in hand, irony in his narrowed eyes
holding in one thought Bosnia, cancer,
persimmons, widows, serial killers,

and you and me in our precarious safety?

7 May 1993

A Report

Hitler, housepainter who painted Warsaw
red, rumored alive in Argentina,

is dead; Stalin defaced; Lenin is a name
for a telephone museum. Vietnam

is a box office hit. Gandhi and King
are black and white photographs smiling

away in bidi shops. They live and die
again and again in followers who buy

potatoes, foreign cars, or just bidis,
changing coins and bills with Kings and Gandhis

stamped on them, seasoned turncoats like our trees
changing colour as new-style biographies

are set in their heroes' bedrooms or campaign
motels. The new dictators hunt, arraign,

and hang the old ones two hours before dawn
unless they flee to Argentina or Bonn,

buy ranches in North Dakota where they
sport gold cufflinks, race horses that neigh

like the Seven Stallions of the Sun, and eat
special fodder vitamined by Vietnamese

cooks and protected by thugs with Uzis.
The very poor in rich spice islands live

now on cocaine harvests and backyard
poppy while Chicago and Zurich have

Needle Parks complete with nurse, priest and guard,
for your daughter or nephew to die in.

A colleague, not gay, not from Benin,
not always in Theater, is terminally

alive with AIDS. Friends visit in anti-
septic plastic suits, dare not kiss or hold

or caress that snake-dry skin, that mould
for a death's-head on a foreign body

once native as a crocodile baby,
frisky, naked, needy, and full of sex.

Yet what can I do, what shall I do, O
god of death and sweet waters under or next

to the salt and the flotsam, what can I do
but sleep, work at love and work, blunder,

sleep again refusing, lest I fall asunder,
to dream of a blue Mysore house in Chicago?

As Eichmann Said, My Brother Said

As Eichmann said, the trains
ran like a dream, my brother said
in the city square and the stocks
were harrumphing bulls on TV.
Towards mountains of spectacles
that had lost their eyes,

gold teeth without faces,
artificial limbs
climbing by themselves
all over the landscape,
junk bonds lying in the graveyard
of cars and caterpillars

all along the train tracks.
As Eichmann said, I obeyed
orders, that's all, my brother
said, and pensions crumbled
as he herded people like himself
into cattle cars, children like his own

into ovens not unlike the ones
in your kitchen, only larger, dying men
making pyramids of tangled hands
and feet, fingers in another's eye,
towards the airhole, the chimney
through which they went up in smoke.

As Eichmann said, how can I
talk about it now
after all these years
of not remembering and not
forgetting either? That was
then, now is now, my brother said.

The Guru

Forgive the weasel his tooth
forgive the tiger his claw

but do not forgive the woman
her malice or the man his envy

said the guru, as he moved on
to ask me to clean his shoe,

bake his bread and wash his clothes.

Give the dog his bone, the parrot
his seed, the pet snake his mouse

but do not give woman her freedom
nor man his midday meal till he begs

said the guru, as he went on
to order his breakfast of eggs and news

asking me to carry his chair to the dais.

I gave the dog his bone, the parrot
his seed, the pet snake his mouse,

forgave the weasel his tooth,
forgave the tiger his claw,

and left the guru to clean his own shoe
for I remembered I was a man born of woman.

251

A Ruler

Governing the country from a kitchen sink
she brandishes ladles as the goddess her sword

puts ministers to work like daughters-in-law
sorting lentils and votes, slicing the gourd

the big white house is hushed when she takes her nap
but caterpillars and mice gnaw holes in the map

Poverty

Poverty is a stranger now.
The mangy dog his friend
stands on two hind legs
with a soup-can in his mouth
to beg with him.

After watching pilgrims
pass him by, poverty blinds
his eyes so his status as a beggar
rises. He breaks the dog's
front legs to raise the pitch

of pity. I knew him once.
On the veranda where I lived
in a blanket, his dog would wake me
with licks on my sleepy face
while he smoked his first bidis.

My eyes wear trifocals
so I can read small print
and large, distinguish
several species of spiders
I'm scared of. My dog

is on a diet
because he has gout.
Poverty is a stranger.

Butcher's Tao

The butcher in China
looks long at a bull till he sees
the bull and how

the beast is jointed,
then moves his knife
in the spaces

he has learned
by heart with his hand
moving on the bull

and the bull
is now sirloin,

tenderloin, prime rib,
dogbone, two horns

for weddings or combs,
sandals for the pedestrian

peasant, saddle and rein
for horse, thong and head

for kettledrums to scare away
eclipses from the sun,

ghosts from processions,
or summon cities

to banquets, friends and
enemies to battle,

the blood in the bucket
ready for sprinkling

on children with polio
and village borders.

A Copper Vat

Sunlit in a museum room,
patina green on copper red,
a vat

large enough for a refugee
to hide in, snakes of brass
for handles,

mouths in their tails, a gargoyle
for a lid, the knob once his nose
worn smooth

by slave girls' hands, the metal
hammered and figured, twined with creeper
and rounded fruit:

picked three centuries ago
by a Portuguese galleon from
a bath house

in Trivandrum, seen just
in passing in a Boston museum
not even by me,

but ten years ago by someone else
who today is someone else
again, why

is it here in a Jerusalem bus,
green patina on red copper,
in a backseat

dream working its way through
a sleet of murmurs and the faces
muffled for winter?

Museum

As people who appear in dreams
are not themselves, the horses
are not horses in the Chinese painting
that prance out of the walls
to trample the flowers
in the emperor's gardens
night after night.

Images

A Taste

Mothers smear bitter neem
paste on their nipples
to wean greedy babies

and give them an inexplicable
taste for bitter gourd
late in life

Slum Crocus

when crocuses poke
blues and yellows through the snow
even slums don't look

away

Invisible Bodies

Just any day, not only after a riot,
even among the gamboge maples of fall
streets are full of bodies, invisible
to the girl under the twirling parasol.

Calcified Type

Why a third white shoe? a spare?
The accountant's eye
sees the world in triplicates.

Others dine. He grubs.
Others live and grow. Mollusc,
he calcifies in rock.

Connections

Brown things unfurl, bloom.
Black breaks out in forsythia.
Even aspirin
capsules ramify
into twig and leaf, explode
into cassia trees.

Spring

Crocuses first, then tulips,
   forsythia, redbud,
dogwood: schoolgirls without coats.

Heart's blood races when Mother
   Goose walks with her row
of chicks through Chicago traffic.

Shut, a fog around the heart.
   Open, the green eyes
of a bicycle woman.

Becoming

Snake and iguana sleep in the sun
looking already polished
like women's wallets and gigolo
shoes, yet afraid of cats and hawks.

Farewell

Mother's farewell had no words,
no tears, only a long look
that moved on your body
from top to toe

with the advice that you should
not forget your oil bath
every tuesday
when you go to America

Tooth

The large tooth in my left jaw
aches: it's mother again
complaining of the large tooth
in her left jaw
the week before she died

Pain

When a man speaks
of pain, he gains merit
if he can speak with irony
and does not move on then
to do what poets

do, i.e., make a poem

Why I Can't Finish this Book

Letting go
of fairytales
is letting go
of what will not
let go:

mother, grandmother
the fat cook
in widow's white
who fed me
rice and ogres

A Life

At three he was sober.
At six he was drunk, a robber
in a fantasy train.

He went on to running naked in the rain,
headed for Paris and the Seine,
whales killed for blubber.

Whipping nightly the natives in rubber
plantations in the folds of his brain
he lived on postcards, nonviolent as a Jain.

Tarantulas

Why do tarantulas crawl
through my stomach skin
when I think of politics?

November

November already
gray, the ivy on redbrick
is all nerves

carpets make your hair
stand on end and doorknobs spark
like a cathode tube

white plumes in woollen
mouths and chimneys, greens grow
wild in children's crayons.

Night's Day

In sleep cripples dance
deafmutes cross-examine the mafia
and cats play hide and seek
with speckled goldfish.

Waking, dancers need crutches
deafmutes and eunuchs
in mafia harems
and piranhas savour cats' flesh.

Lies

The newborn was ugly, moist
hairy all over like a wet rat:
every visitor said
she was a beauty,
had her mother's eyes.

In Toyland

In bins of rubber
chameleon, the live one
mimics the mimics.

Yellow flecks on green
on a green and yellow bush,
but for a moving

eye:

'If you think you see
nothing on a tree, then it's
a chameleon you see'.

On Learning

The pillow's a sack
knobbed with potatoes. The whorls
on the fingers turn.

Unlearn the body's
old ways. Govern the wavering
lines towards a face,

a walking waking
figures out there in the window
under the trees.

Zero

The Mayans had a glyph for zero
he said

The Hindus thought zero was holy
I said

The Jewish god was one, the Buddhist was zero
he said

Take away the zero from zero it's still zero
I said

zero has no value until it follows a real number
he said

Like you, me and this talk
I said

If Eyes Can See

A poor man's history will brown the gold
of day as mere air browns a cut apple.
Green moss muffles the steps of a childhood
house. Doors and windows open into cobwebs.

A family once lived there with pictures
on the wall, women in the kitchen, a yard
noisy with children, men working in the woods,
reading newspapers in the verandahs.

A change of government, embezzlement in a bank,
a law that parcelled the land to cousins,
and sheer fecklessness have crumbled the walls,
messed up the children, auctioned the pictures.

Yet days can be golden, apples beautiful,
if eyes can see only days and apples.

Elegy

a grown son's tears in a restaurant mix their salt
with a colleague's long-awaited sudden
death in Jodhpur

the breath of garlic as we enter
the elevator suffocates me
for this colleague

chewed on twelve garlic cloves every morning
as a cure for cancer after
an amputation

quoted Keats on the sparrow in the sun
the grape pressed into his palate
believed in homeopathic

doses of cowdung Shelley's chemical
experiments and the calcium deficiency
of his high-pitched verse

how native doctors had little white pills
for homesickness abroad how they
diagnosed your liver

and kidney by seeing whether your urine
stream was one or divided
in two did you know

it was not Wordsworth but his sister
who heard the solitary reaper
by which time

the elevator had reached the eighteenth floor
and I'd to get out and sign a health
insurance form

unable to shake off the whiff of garlic or
the taste of the grape now round
now crushed

in the mouth of Keats in the mouth
of my friend who had mixed them
into my breath

15 January 1992

Lines

Who's this out there
with your face and not your hair?
Images detached from mirrors
float through the room,
cross minds and corridors,
come between you and the shadow
on the wall. That's when
you see her, or is it him,
with your nose but not your brow.
Your wife asks, 'What has happened
to you? Did you get a haircut?'
For the invisible things you see
affect your looks, the form
and not the shape of your face.
His, or is it her, parts
are yours, but they do not add up
to who you are, and you too
are no longer you.
Sometimes, the other when
she's a woman, walks with a left-
foot shuffle and turns around
a quarter-circle when afraid
just like you.
Clones subtly gone wrong
make you wrong, unmake your sense,
change your toilet habits
as if you're in a different time
zone, you develop knots
in your fingers and you feel
sudden streaks of orange heat
across your chest.

6 December 1991

To a Friend Far Away

Between official letters, I doodle the wet
wild tendrils of a familiar alphabet:

I leaf through telephone books, watch the sand
run as I read small print inked on your hand:

breathing the sulphur of city fumes,
I sense your faraway breathing rhythms

quicken as you turn round and round
looking for a child in the market crowd:

hear oceans lash between now and now,
groping in the mist for what I can know,

do, or be, when affections find a bird,
tiny, button-eyed, city-bewildered,

green-yellow, hopping in the yard: I take it
home in a kerchief to a checkered blanket

maybe only to find it dead
by morning in the twist and fold

of my confusions, my absent presence,
faraway rivers amok in my continents.

10 March 1993

Some Monarchs and a Wish

The ancients thought
these gorgeous monarchs
gorge themselves on butter.
Nightingales and larks
have apt names. They sing
when they are young.
But a butterfly
is a slip of the tongue
for 'flutter by'.

Worse than Chicago bag
ladies, under a microscope
they are gluttonous monsters,
eyes without pupils, antennae
coiled whips with rows
of teeth: no less than the sexy
and the young, they zigzag
through our quotidian day
and sober our sense
of the beautiful. Only crows
fly straight.

In a single season, eggs
that dot the leaves turn
into caterpillars, hairy,
obtuse, on tiny elephant legs,
all mouth and green blood,
they live to eat several times
their bodies' weight, die into cocoons
hung-up on being dead
for a while, a delicacy

waiting on the inmost
miracle, a change of heart,
a flight of the psyche
on paper wings
tearing the artifice
of a short-lived body
for another transience,
making out of flowers
colors that rival
the flowers, weaving
refractions of common
or garden light
into iridiscence
like soap bubbles or oil-
slick on the beaches:
as we read them
we read ourselves
in that wish come true,
a kind of aging
loveliest at the end,

oblique as a wit
among invaginate flowers,
insinuating aerial sex,
seminal by proxy,
emperors without politics
or empire, flying upwind
towards the scent
of females equally old
and caught, driven
by metamorphic miracles.

Having died once,
a second death can be an act
of consummate pleasure.

(after reading Primo Levi on butterflies)

From Where?

When, well or ill, the task is done,
the images lose their spin,
lose their hum, as they wobble, roll, lie still,

I ask, where did they come from?

From the mice and the murder clues
in the subterranean granaries I house
but do not own? from the fights

over blue kindergarten kites and my very first

thought of Human Rights, caught in a gale
in '33, a tangle in a neem tree
on New Year's Day? From watching Mother

watching her trellis, green inchworms arching

their backs in '39 from peapod
to desolate peapod, when I'd just heard
of the World and Hitler's packs? Or is it

like the anticipation of a look

in your eyes right now, streaked with turquoise
in the sequins of Sicily seas
far back in '65, May 14,

cutting across the bangles broken

on mother's hour of widowhood, things taken
for lost like Father and his unspoken dying
thought in the fruit market in '53,

and mixing the face of Chaudhuri,

our Hindi man, burned to cinders last week
in a burning wood as he turned back to see
where all the fleeing wild mice came from?

24 October 1989

Death in Search of a Comfortable Metaphor

Grandmother's version
of how scorpions die
to give birth
may not be true
but sounds right.

Maybe death is such
a scorpion: bursts its back
and gives birth
to numerous dying things,
baby scorpions,

terrifying intricate
beauties, interlocked
in male and female,
to eat, grow, sting,
multiply, burst their backs

in turn, and become feasts
of fodder for working
ants, humus for elephant
grasses that become elephants
that leave their herds
to die grand lonely deaths.

But when did elephants
console the living
left behind by a death?

16 March 1992
[the poet's sixty-third birthday]

Pain

Pains in my ankle flicker, nerve ends
glower and dim like cigarette ends
in a chain smoker's mouth night and day.

Doctors X-ray the foot, front face and back,
left profile and right as if for a police
file, unearth shadow fossils of neanderthals
buried in this contemporary foot;
they draw three test tubes of blood as I turn
my face away, and label my essences
with a mis-spelled name; put my body whole
into a white tunnel with no light
at the end, inject a green dayglo liquid
to take pictures in dots of purple
and sickly pink on a computer screen.
Men and women of different races
and sizes in white smocks look at the dots
and shake their heads.

The pain in the ankle glowers on, a red-hot
coal pressed now and then against a nerve
nobody can find.

O god of knowledge, busy wizard
of diagnosis, father of needles, dials,
and test tubes, send your old companion here,
that mother of mothers, goddess though of ignorance,
send her soon so she can kiss away my pain
as she has always done.

12 December 1992; 11 April 1993

Fear No Fall

1

Arunagiri, rich and spoiled, spent
his youth and old money,
heirlooms and a sister's dowry
on medieval liquors, honeymead and coconutarrack,
pressing Arab wineskins into his mouth
in coastal shipyards,

and on women

till one of them sucked him dry
of all his juices,
gave him syphilitic sores
in all the wrong places,
and threw him out, a peel of many colors
on the garbage heap.

Unhoused, he roamed

through the town, a target
for moralists' fingers,
a lesson for future generations,
dripping with diseases
for which they had no names yet
though quacks offered arsenic and antidotes.

His despair deeper than his wounds,

he struggled with bush and rubble
up a cliff, surveyed the world
he had lost in the valleys
of light and shadow, towers
and gardens and treetops,
and just threw himself down.

Yet he woke up, strangely unsurprised,

Arunagiri: a Tamil saint

smooth and whole again in every limb,
lying in the lap of a very old man
who smiled at him, wrinkled,
through white hair on a dark
face, ten white strands
on his chin like a Chinese sage,

who said to him, 'Sing now of Murugan!'

Arunagiri, truant extraordinary,
escape artist, burglar of hearts,
guzzler on all good things,
who didn't have an alphabet
in his past nor ever a tune in his head,
hated temple bells and hypocrisies,

asked, 'How can I? Unlettered, worthless?'

The old man who was really the Old Man
of the oldest Novas, gave him his first line
of verse, and while Arunagiri
turned it round and round like candy
in his mouth, new lines forming
all around the Old One, the Old Man

melted away like a figure in a fog,

leaving Arunagiri a lifetime
of seeking and finding and losing Him
again and again in a labyrinth
of winding words, his songs
twining around trees, ensnaring
passersby, unlocking cages

even for mynahs and parrots.

2

That night
I was tottering without a foothold
on a ramshackle pyramid
of all my books piled any which way
on to a horse cart
and me slipping on top of it,
without a door or a wall to my name,
moving through a market town,
looking for a place,
dropping books in several languages
all along the way,
in a panic fear of falling and breaking my neck
in the gutters below
when a voice both within and without
said, 'Fall, fall,
you'll never fear a fall again,
fall now!'

A *Note on* The Black Hen *and After*

Eight writers helped select the poems in *The Black Hen*, roughly about half the total number of poems that the poet had entered into his computer.

The poems were never composed directly on the computer. They started in the journal, were written by hand, revised many times, and finally transferred in a nearly finished state to the computer. All of the one hundred and forty-eight poems were publishable, but it would have been a disproportionate size compared to the earlier three volumes. Therefore, it was decided that the remaining poems could be published later in a volume of uncollected poems.

Each of the four books in *The Collected Poems* has a characteristic Ramanujan quality. At the same time each book has its own identity. The difference between *The Black Hen* and the earlier books helped give the selection its coherence and its distinction. It seemed at first that the poems could be read very fast, but that was only a surface impression. Soon it became evident that these poems needed repeated reading, as they had a cumulative effect and added up to four or five interrelated themes. The editors found that each poem yielded more at each reading. The task of ranking the poems and then arranging the order of the poems was challenging, to say the very least.

In his *Selected Poems* (1976), the poet placed 'Epitaph on a Street Dog' opposite 'A Hindu to his Body,' thereby lighting up both poems. Such ironic juxtaposition could have been attempted here, but instead, we tried to strike a balance between extremes, resisting the temptation to be too paradoxical, or too obvious in arranging the order of the poems.

Ever the Keatsian chameleon, in the final sixth of his life Ramanujan could forge contraries to recreate a world in which he could, like his salamanders, find birth in death and death in birth. He prayed for double vision and found it in the intercon-

278

nectedness of vegetable and mineral, man and animal. Above all, he found life-in-art and art-in-life.

Nothing is simple in these poems: the seeming simplicity is deceptive. For example, in the title poem, 'The Black Hen', a *maker* (poet) looking at what he has created becomes terrified. This idea is further extended in the poem, 'Museum.' The horses in a Chinese painting have a nocturnal power. They 'prance' out of the wall and with uncanny ability are able to strike their target 'night after night'. They seem to be imbued with the compulsiveness of a repetitive dream. This seven-line poem is a striking example of the poet's view of creativity:

> As people who appear in dreams
> are not themselves, the horses
> are not horses in the Chinese painting
> that prance out of the walls
> to trample the flowers
> in the emperor's gardens
> night after night.

The poem begins with the words, 'As people who appear in dreams / are not themselves', as if this were a known fact. In doing so, the poet is tethering the rest of the poem to an unprovable assumption as if it were proven.

He introduces the 'as' clause without fanfare and speedily pushes ahead. The idea of horses jumping out of the canvases may be a Chinese notion, but the use he puts it to is quite astonishingly his own. The action of the horses is tied to what happens in repetitive dreams. The dissenting reader, who might have wanted to stop and think about the logic of the dependent clause, is caught and pushed ahead by the twin sides of the comparison, the people in dreams and the horses in a painting.

If the 'people' who 'appear in dreams' are *not themselves*, they must have had an identity prior to their appearance in the dream, and an existence where they *are themselves*. Logic outside the poem wants to say: Look here, how can you imply that people *are themselves* outside the dream? And yet, the poem compels us to reread till we begin to see.

It could be said that either the dreamer or the dream itself has refracted or deflected 'the people who appear in dreams' to become *not-themselves*, and likewise, the horses in the Chinese painting are *not-horses*. Obviously there is a difference between the refraction or the deflection of persons from that of horses. The horses are *not-horses*, unlike the humans who are *not-themselves*. The poem has a human perspective.

And yet, if they are not horses, then why do they 'prance' as only horses can? Obviously they are horse enough, but something else too. Perhaps the people who appear in dreams are sufficiently themselves to be recognized as such. The horses in the painting seem to have a repetitive compulsion, a nocturnal one, of coming off the museum walls and destroying 'the flowers / in the emperor's gardens / night after night'.

Flowers in an emperor's garden are obviously quite different from flowers in nature. Not quite like flowers in, say, meadowland. The emperor's gardens are tended by a gardener who makes artistic arrangements of something natural. One assumes that the flowers are flowers, and therefore different from the *not-horses* and the people who are *not themselves*.

However, in the action of the poem, by destroying the flowers night after night, shouldn't we assume that it is happening not in the actual world of power and politics, but somewhere in the same region as where dreams exist? But since more words are used for the painting than for the dream, the poem is saying something about art and life.

In life, the poet believed in a Jungian interpretation of all dreams. Accordingly, if all the parts of the dream were the dreamer himself, then the subjects and objects within the dream and the painting are all parts of the dreamer or the artist. The flowers no less than the horses are part of the artist's world. The terror in the poem is the artist's terror, of parts of his work creating havoc night after night, wrecking the flowers in the gardens.

If 'The Black Hen' leans towards singulars, the 'Museum' contains plurals. The flowers in the gardens could stand for the many things the *maker* values outside of his art. If we were to use paradigms for flowers, i.e., pets, children, and friends, we would get the scale of his life. But if we were to play a literary game and allude to another poem on poetry—Marianne Moore's 'imaginary gardens' with 'real toads' in them, or inversely, real 'gardens' with imaginary 'toads' in them—the scale would relate to his life as a poet. For Ramanujan, the real and the imaginary are as inseparable as the Yeatsian 'dancer' and 'the dance'. This goes further for Ramanujan. For him, the 'dance' itself remembers the 'dancer'.

We now see why the people in dreams, and the nocturnal acts of destruction of the *not-horses*, are correlated. By making the introductory dependent clause the axis of his poem, the poet arrests our attention and presents a metaphorical truth. The making of a painting no less than the making of a dream shares a terrifying obsessive destructive power in the life of the *maker*. Etymologically *poet* and *maker* are interchangeable, but the act of creation entails a putting together and pulling apart. 'The Black Hen' and 'Museum' are two of several poems about such cycles in life and in art. Poem speaks to poem, and we eavesdroppers begin to develop yet another layer of meaning.

Because of their interconnectedness, the compilers of this book found it hard to rank the poems. No selection is perfect, and each reader felt consoled by the thought that the poems not included here will be published later. In publishing this posthumous book of poems close to the first anniversary of the poet's death, they are wishing his spirit release, they are wishing him completion.

Molly Daniels-Ramanujan

Index of Titles

Index of First Lines